DISCOVER
NATURAL
MISSOURI

❧

A Guide to Exploring

The Nature Conservancy Preserves

Printed in the United States of America.

The Nature Conservancy,
Missouri Chapter
2800 S. Brentwood Blvd.
St. Louis, Missouri 63144
(314) 968-1105

ACKNOWLEDGMENTS

Many talented people have worked on different aspects of this guide over the past year. The preserve descriptions were written by Doug Ladd, Mike Nolan, Margaret Clancy, and Robyn Flakne, all staff of the Missouri Chapter of The Nature Conservancy, and edited by Lee Fox of The Fox Group. ❧ The maps were drawn by Belinka Held, a dedicated volunteer. ❧ The photographs appear through the generosity of many photographers: Conservancy trustee Robert Lindholm, Kiku Obata, Dr. Harold Malde, Dr. Jeffrey Graves, Steve Tomey, Kay Yatskievych, Sherry Morgan, Bill Summers, and the Missouri Department of Conservation. ❧ The line drawings from the "Illustrated Flora of Illinois" series are reprinted courtesy of Dr. Robert H. Mohlenbrock and Southern Illinois University Press. Paul Nelson created the line drawing of *geocarpon minimum*. ❧ Dennis Figg, Endangered Species Coordinator at the Missouri Department of Conservation, researched, wrote, and provided photographs. Thanks also to Leslie Warren, Larry Mechlin, Tom Toney, and George Yatskievych at the Department of Conservation. ❧ It would not have been possible to create a preserve guide this comprehensive without the generous financial support of Intoximeters and Malt-O-Meal corporations, and Mrs. Anne Lehmann, who helped underwrite the costs. ❧ Finally, our thanks to Kiku Obata, Teresa Bollwerk, and Patty Kennedy of Kiku Obata & Company, who designed and produced the book. ❧

TABLE OF CONTENTS

Foreword

by Peter H. Raven, Director, Missouri Botanical Garden

State Map

THE MISSION OF

THE NATURE CONSERVANCY

IS TO PRESERVE PLANTS, ANIMALS,

AND NATURAL COMMUNITIES THAT REPRESENT

THE DIVERSITY OF LIFE ON EARTH

BY PROTECTING THE LANDS AND WATER

THEY NEED TO SURVIVE.

THE NATURE CONSERVANCY BELIEVES

THERE IS STILL TIME TO PRESERVE

THE NATURAL WORLD—THE

RARE WILDLIFE, THE SPECIAL PLACES.

IT IS NOT TOO LATE—YET.

FOREWORD

*M*issouri stands alone among mid-western states for the variety and diversity of its natural communities. No less than six major natural divisions exist in the state, each with a distinct assemblage of plant and animal species.

What forces led to the occurrence of this diversity in such a limited area? In large measure, it is a function of the state's geology and position on the continent. The Ozark Mountains represent the oldest continuously exposed landscape in the world. Now heavily dissected into twisting valleys of many rock types, the Ozarks host different microclimates, depending on such factors as the trend of a valley, the abundance of water, and the composition of the bedrock and soil. The regional climate, which has changed radically over the past 20,000 years, has produced a series of very different biological communities that have persisted locally in favorable habitats.

Parts of Missouri are relatively flat. The tall-grass prairie of northern Missouri grows on land that was glaciated. The rolling prairies of the southwestern portion of the state grow on soils that weren't glaciated, *and that are dryer. The big rivers have created deep, productive soils from their silt.*

Over the millennia, ecosystems in Missouri have adapted to these soil types, these weather variations, and the relative abundance of water. Nearly 100 individual natural communities have been identified by scientists throughout the state.

Although distinctive, Missouri's ecosystems do not stand alone. Each grades into natural communities outside the state, and eventually outside the country. All these ecosystems interconnect through their role in the global climate, their habitat for migratory animals, and the unique niche filled by the different species. The loss of these natural communities—through urban development, farming, logging, mining, and road building—is perhaps the single most critical problem facing the world today.

Ten years ago, Harvard biologist Edward O. Wilson warned "The one process ongoing in the 1980s that will take millions of years to correct is the loss of genetic and species diversity by the destruction of natural habitats. This is the folly our descendants are least likely to forgive us."

The rate of extinction is increasing worldwide, and the main cause is the destruction of habitat and natural communities. If we don't speed up the preservation of natural habitats or face the possibility that plant and animal species will soon be lost, piece by piece, our natural heritage will dwindle beyond recovery.

We must preserve natural areas and the diversity of life they support. The Nature Conservancy has developed a method of doing just that, protecting over 5 million acres throughout this hemisphere over the last forty years. Their system of nature preserves is perhaps the best hope—and for some natural communities, maybe the only hope—for the long-term protection of endangered plant and animal species.

Now we must speed up the process. What hasn't been saved by the year 2000 may be lost forever.

Extinction is final, but there is still time to make a difference. A visit to a Nature Conservancy preserve shows what can be done with dedication to the task.

Peter H. Raven

Director, Missouri Botanical Garden

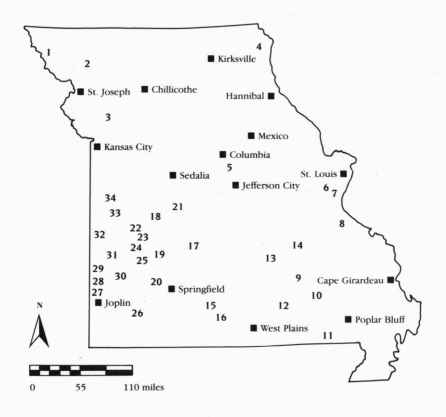

1. Kirksville
2. St. Joseph
Chillicothe
Hannibal
3. Kansas City
Mexico
Columbia
Sedalia
Jefferson City
St. Louis
34
33
21
32
22
23
24
31
19
17
14
29
13
28
30
9
Cape Girardeau
27
20
Springfield
10
Joplin
15
12
26
16
West Plains
Poplar Bluff

N

0   55   110 miles

1. Jamerson C. McCormack Loess Mounds
2. Dobbins Woodland
3. Trice-Dedman Memorial Woods
4. Accola Woods
5. Hinkson Valley
6. Nancy B. Altvater LaBarque Hills
7. Victoria Glade
8. Silas Dees Azalea and Wildflower
9. Nancy B. Altvater Grasshopper Hollow
10. Lily Pond

11. Nancy B. Altvater Pondberry Preserve
12. Nancy B. Altvater Shut-In Mountain Fens
13. Hyer Woods
14. Zahorsky Woods
15. Alma Peterson Azalea Memorial
16. N. L. Williams Memorial Woods
17. Bennett Spring Savanna
18. Lichen Glade
19. Nancy B. Altvater Corry Flatrocks
20. Greenfield Glade

21. Rockhill Prairie
22. Wah 'Kon-Tah Prairie
23. Mo-Ko Prairie
24. Monegaw Prairie
25. Niawathe Prairie
26. Mount Vernon Prairie
27. Wah-Sha-She Prairie
28. Hunkah Prairie
29. Tzi-Sho Prairie
30. Shelton L. Cook Memorial Meadow
31. Pawhuska Prairie
32. Little Osage Prairie
33. Marmaton River Bottoms Wet Prairie
34. Gamagrass Meadows

Missouri Nature Conservancy Preserves

INTRODUCTION

When European settlers began arriving in Missouri in the first part of the nineteenth century, they found a vastly different place than one finds today. Missouri was comprised of enormous, sprawling prairies, vast forests, magnificent wild rivers, and an abundant variety of plants and animals.

This beautiful land, with its wealth of resources, was a strong magnet for the thousands of new Americans who were looking for a better life for themselves and their children. They came to Missouri to farm, to mine, to hunt, to cut timber, and to build roads, cities, and industries. In the process they changed Missouri forever.

Very little of Missouri remains as it was prior to settlement in the 1800s. At The Nature Conservancy's Missouri preserves, you can still glimpse the natural heritage that has sustained and nurtured the state, but that is now quickly being lost.

This book introduces thirty-four nature preserves in Missouri. These preserves are the creation of The Nature Conservancy, an international nonprofit environmental organization. The Conservancy's single mission is to find, protect, and maintain the best examples of rare and endangered species and natural communities in the world. Using a variety of protection methods, the Conservancy has quietly acquired more than 8,500 parcels of ecologically important land scattered throughout the United States, the Caribbean, and Latin America.

In Missouri, The Nature Conservancy began its protection activities in 1957, when a small group of dedicated volunteers successfully concluded negotiations to purchase Tucker Prairie, just east of Columbia. Since then, more than 36,000 acres have been protected through outright purchase, through donations and exchanges, and by lease and easement.

The number of known potential projects increased with the establishment of the Natural Features Inventory in 1981 and demanded the attention of a professional staff. In 1982, the Missouri Field Office opened in St. Louis. Its first project was the protection of 568 acres at Marmaton River Bottoms Wet Prairie in Vernon County. Since then, the Field Office has gone on to protect more than 9,500 acres at twenty-six additional sites.

But acquiring the land is only the beginning of the job. The Nature Conservancy also plays an active role in managing many of the areas they acquire. Staff ecologists make regular visits to each preserve to check on the overall health of the natural communities present and to ensure that the most-endangered species can survive successfully.

Stewardship entails a myriad of activities. Preserve boundaries must be fenced and signed, trails built and maintained, trash removed, and non-native exotic plants eliminated. One of the most spectacular of the stewardship activities is the reintroduction of fire to ecosystems that are sustained by it. The Conservancy relies heavily on its active membership to help maintain its preserves (nearly 7,000 Missourians are members), and volunteers are recruited for the majority of the routine stewardship activity.

The Nature Conservancy's lands are open to the public and visitation is encouraged. This book will guide you to the Conservancy's preserves around the state. Each preserve description provides an overview of the preserve's natural history and an explanation of what makes it unique. Every description is followed by a map and detailed directions to the area.

When you visit a preserve, remember to bring field guides, binoculars, and a magnifying glass. During the summer months expect to find both ticks and chiggers, often in abundance. Summers can be extremely hot and humid, so plan to explore slowly—sometimes the most beautiful and rare features are the less obvious.

After you've visited the site, consider supporting The Nature Conservancy. The Conservancy is funded entirely by private funds, eighty percent of which comes from individuals. Your support, and that of thousands of other Americans, will ensure that what can be saved, will be saved—now. We will never have a second chance. ❧

JAMERSON C. MCCORMACK LOESS MOUNDS

Located in extreme northwestern Missouri, in one of the most geologically fascinating and botanically unique areas of the Midwest, McCormack Loess Mounds Preserve is one of Missouri's premiere natural areas.

The Conservancy's portion of the McCormack Loess Mounds Preserve was donated by Jamerson C. McCormack, a St. Louis resident and prudent conservationist who had owned the site for many years. The Missouri Department of Conservation acquired additional acreage adjacent to the Conservancy donation. Today, a total of 227 combined acres are protected at the preserve. The site is jointly managed through close cooperation between The Nature Conservancy and the Department of Conservation.

Loess (pronounced "luss") mounds are unique, grass-dominated natural communities known only from northwestern Missouri, eastern Nebraska, western Iowa, and southeastern South Dakota. They are most prominent along the Missouri River, where they form steep ridges oriented in a north-south direction. These sharp-textured hills form intricate ridge and valley matrices and lend an angular, jagged appearance to the landscape.

Many of the plants and animals at McCormack Loess Mounds are more characteristic of the Great Plains. In addition to the native prairie grasses and forbs that dominate the area, several species found here are members of disjunct populations where closest relatives occur hundreds of miles to the west. These include downy painted cup, low milk vetch, skeleton plant, and plains pocket mouse; all are endangered in Missouri. Other special plants at the site include thimbleweed, rock satin grass, and dalea.

Despite their rugged appearance, the loess mounds are among the most fragile of ecosystems. They lack the underlying rock layers that typically make up hilly regions and as a result are extremely susceptible to erosion. The silty loess soils are excessively well drained, especially on south and west slopes, which are continually exposed to the sun and prevailing winds; only drought-tolerant plants survive here. As you walk through the preserve, notice how the vegetation varies according to aspect. Woody plants tend to occur on the cool, moist north and east slopes, while hardy prairie plants dominate the drier sites. Notice that these prairie plants have special adaptations such as tiny, narrow leaves or densely hairy stems to help them conserve water. These species are finely tuned to their loess hills environment.

The steep terrain at McCormack makes for some difficult hiking, and visitors should be prepared for rigorous climbing. The trail from the parking area takes you up through some of the woody areas into the prairie openings above. Partway up, the trail

forks and the left-hand spur leads to a scenic overlook with spectacular views of the Missouri River valley. A lookout platform at the end
of the trail provides an excellent place to observe birds and other
wildlife. The right-hand spur ascends sharply and eventually takes
you to the eastern edge of the property. Visitors are urged to use
extreme caution when venturing off the trail. Take a map and compass and be especially mindful of the fragile nature of the land.

A complete tour of the McCormack Preserve takes at least half
a day but is well worth it. Bring binoculars and a wildflower guide
and try to identify a few of the unique plants and animals here. The
Missouri Department of Conservation and The Nature Conservancy
have used a variety of management techniques to try to restore
some prairie areas and control weed invasion. Since the time of the
original land survey of the area, a significant amount of prairie has
been lost to woody encroachment, mostly by rough-leaved dogwood, which forms dense thickets. To date, much of the management has been centered on testing the effects of prescribed burning
at different times of the year in an attempt to restore the presettlement prairie. Soil erosion is being measured to determine what
effect it may have on the survival of the ecosystems here.

JAMERSON C. MCCORMACK LOESS MOUNDS

Holt County ❧ *158 Acres*

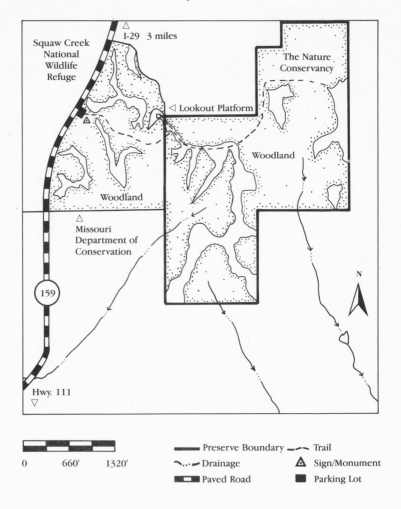

Squaw Creek National Wildlife Refuge

I-29   3 miles

The Nature Conservancy

◁ Lookout Platform

Woodland

Woodland

Missouri Department of Conservation

159

N

Hwy. 111

| 0 | 660' | 1320' |

Preserve Boundary

Drainage

Paved Road

Trail

Sign/Monument

Parking Lot

AT A GLANCE

LOCATION

About five miles due south of Mound City, Missouri on Highway 159 (Sec. 31, T61N, R38W, Holt County).

DIRECTIONS

From the junction of Highway 159 and Interstate 29 south of Mound City, head west on Highway 159 for three miles. A sign for the preserve and parking lot are on the east side of the road here.

USGS TOPO MAP

Kimsey Creek 7.5 minute quadrangle.

PROTECTED NATURAL FEATURES

Natural Community: *Loess hill prairie.*
Species: *Downy painted cup, low milk vetch, skeleton plant, thimbleweed, rock satin grass, dalea, plains pocket mouse.*

BEST TIME TO GO

Spring and fall are probably best, although any time is good for a visit.

HIKING CONDITIONS

Steep terrain. Rigorous hiking and plenty of climbing.

2

DOBBINS WOODLAND

Little woodland exists today in far northwestern Missouri. Dobbins Woodland, forty acres of gently rolling uplands dissected by small stream valleys, provides a needed refuge for some woodland plants and animals in the region. This site has been preserved through a partial donation from the Dobbins family, whose ancestors settled here in the 1800s.

A variety of canopy trees occur here. Black walnut, hackberry, bitternut hickory and elm are found on the bottomlands along the stream courses. Red oak, shagbark hickory, red mulberry, and elm can be seen on the moist midslopes. The oak-hickory association continues on the uplands, with white oak, black oak, and chinquapin oak as additional trees.

During mid spring, a profusion of spring wildflowers creates scenic panoramas on the wooded slopes. Typical spring flora here include violets, toothwort, jack-in-the-pulpit, wild geranium, Virginia waterleaf, and spiderwort. Ferns at the site include maidenhair fern, fragile fern, and scouring rush. Other plants include the Indian pipe, a pure white plant incapable of producing its own food, Kentucky coffee tree, and yellow giant hyssop.

Over one hundred species of birds have been documented in the preserve, including scarlet tanager, rose-breasted grosbeak,

great crested flycatcher, and indigo bunting. Spring migration brings warblers to the woods, among them chestnut sided, magnolia, yellow-rumped, bay breasted, palm, Nashville, and golden winged warblers. Mammals documented from Dobbins Woodland include coyote, raccoon, white-tailed deer, and red fox as well as moles, pine voles, evening bats, red bats, and big brown bats.

Although the site has experienced some disturbance since settlement, it remains an island of significant natural quality in the largely agricultural landscape of northwestern Missouri. Northwest Missouri State University uses the area for research and assists with management and monitoring.

DOBBINS WOODLAND

Nodaway County 🙚 *40 Acres*

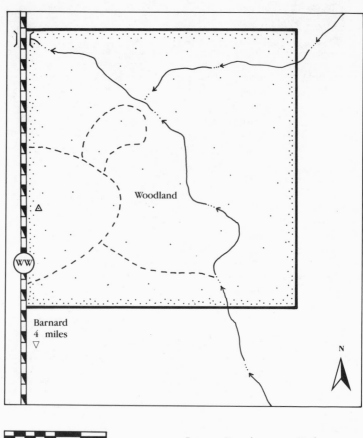

LOCATION	*In extreme northwestern Missouri, approximately five miles north of Barnard (Sec. 26, T63N, R35W, Nodaway County).*
DIRECTIONS	*From the junction of Highways M and WW in the small town of Barnard, proceed north on WW for approximately 4.3 miles, where WW ends. Continue straight north on a dirt road for about a quarter mile, until the preserve sign is visible on the right. Dobbins Woodland lies south of the stream and east of the road.*
USGS TOPO MAP	*Bolckow 15 minute quadrangle.*
PROTECTED NATURAL FEATURES	**Natural Communities**: *Mesic bottomland forest, mesic upland forest, dry-mesic upland forest.* **Species**: *Indian pipe, spring wildflowers, over 100 bird species.*
BEST TIME TO GO	*Mid spring for spring wildflowers, late spring for migrating warblers, and fall to view the colorful foliage.*
HIKING CONDITIONS	*Slopes are moderate and walking is fairly easy; insect repellent is desirable at times.*

3

TRICE-DEDMAN WOODS

Twenty five miles north of Kansas City lies a small but impressive remnant of the oak timbers that once wove through the prairies of northwestern Missouri. Trice-Dedman Woods is a sixty-acre remnant of an old growth oak woodland, donated to the Conservancy by Mary Ellen and Rebecca Dedman in honor of their families' active protection of the site for over a century.

Most of the preserve lies north of Highway 116 between Platts-burg and Lathrop. A two-mile hiking trail leads through most of the area. The landscape here is characterized by gentle, rolling slopes, with infrequent boulders and low outcrops of limestone bedrock in valley bottoms and stream courses. For much of its length, the trail is through an impressive stand of large white oaks, with occasional hickories and infrequent bur, post, and black oaks. Most of the large white oaks are 160 to 180 years old. Under-story trees are largely maple, elm, ironwood, and hickory. More than 200 native plant species grow at the site.

A favorite time to visit the site is spring, when the profusion of violets, spring beauties, Dutchman's breeches, and trout lilies creates a colorful spectacle. More diligent searchers will be re-warded by sightings of orchids, dwarf larkspur, early horse gentian, yellow honeysuckle, and green dragon. Birders will appreciate the profusion of warblers and other migrants visiting Trice-Dedman Woods during the spring migration.

One management concern at Trice-Dedman Woods is the lack of reproduction and recruitment into the canopy of many of the typical canopy oaks. Instead, studies have demonstrated that the canopy oaks are being replaced by more shade tolerant maples and elms, causing concern for the long term continued existence of the site. A look at the 1819 land survey notes for the area is even more revealing: the woodland was bordered within one half mile on two sides by open, treeless prairie, and half of the witness trees were bur oak, half white oak. There is no mention of maple, ironwood, or elm within a mile of the site in any direction. Average distance to a witness tree was more than fifty feet.

Certainly, this is a different woodland than exists at the site today. Another clue to the original nature of the site is revealed by the presence of plants such as Culver's root, yellow pimpernel, purple milkweed, tickseed coreopsis, and Michigan lily. These plants, typically associated with more open or savanna-like woodlands, are rare at the site, and generally do not flower, but remain as stunted vegetative individuals. Since such plants are restricted in their habitat requirements, and generally incapable of spreading into new areas, they are almost certainly survivors from the formerly more open woodland that prevailed at the site. Under current conditions, the profusion of young elms and maples has largely shaded out the ground level, supplanting the diverse woodland flora in all but small openings and along trails.

In order to assure that future generations will be able to enjoy this remnant oak woodland, Conservancy management activities at the site are centered around efforts to restore its original character. We are testing the use of controlled fire to emulate the Indian-set fires that were pervasive in Missouri prior to European settlement. As you hike the trail, you will walk through a small research fire unit just across the foot bridge. Note that the increased light and relative lack of understory have resulted in a better developed and more diverse ground cover vegetation than elsewhere in the woods.

While much remains to be learned about Missouri woodlands and their management, areas such as Trice-Dedman Woods are starting to provide some insights into Missouri's unique and diverse woodland systems. As a place to get away from the pressures of modern life and glimpse a fragment of "original Missouri," it is a beautiful, tranquil window to our natural heritage.

TRICE-DEDMAN MEMORIAL WOODS

Clinton County ❧ *60 Acres*

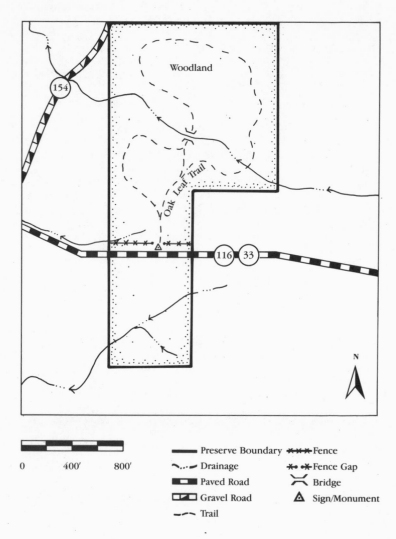

0   400'   800'

— Preserve Boundary   ✳✳✳ Fence
➤··➤ Drainage   ✳·✳ Fence Gap
▰▱ Paved Road   ⏝ Bridge
▰▱ Gravel Road   △ Sign/Monument
--⌒ Trail

LOCATION

Approximately three miles east of Plattsburg along Highway 116 (Sec. 20, T55N, R31W, Clinton County).

DIRECTIONS

From Plattsburg, proceed east on Highway 116 for approximately two miles, then another 0.7 miles, parking in small pull-in along north side of road, next to preserve sign. Trail loop starts here.

USGS
TOPO MAP

Plattsburg 7.5 minute quadrangle.

PROTECTED
NATURAL
FEATURES

Natural Community: *Old growth oak woodland (dry mesic upland forest).*
Species: *ferns, three species of orchids, unusual sedges, spring wildflowers, migrating warblers.*

BEST TIME
TO GO

Spring for wildflowers and birds, summer for lush woodland vistas and shaded trail, and fall to view colorful foliage.

HIKING
CONDITIONS

Well-marked trail, with moderate to gentle slopes, and readily accessible. No special clothing or gear is necessary. Repellent is suggested.

4

ACCOLA WOODS

At Accola Woods in Lewis County, The Nature Conservancy is preserving one of northeastern Missouri's rarest community types. A donation from Carl Accola, this forty-acre woodland is believed to be a remnant of the swamp white oak savanna that once characterized much of the local landscape.

Accola Woods contains a unique assemblage of trees and herbaceous plants that are testimony to the land's past. Here, large, widely-spaced oaks and hickories with spreading crowns dominate the overstory, while grasses, sedges, and other prairie-like forbs dot the ground layer. Most of these ground dwelling species were probably prolific in the understory prior to settlement. Today they persist in vegetative (non-flowering) forms or in reduced numbers, having to compete for light and soil nutrients with the second growth maple and elm poles that have invaded the site. Generations of post-settlement alterations have also resulted in a dense growth of buckbrush over large portions of the site, further shading much of the ground layer.

Fortunately, Accola Woods has retained some of its biological diversity; over 200 native species occur here. Green dragon, purple spring cress, golden seal, downy arrow-wood, and yellow honeysuckle are typical plants flowering at the site in early spring and summer. Rare plants at the site, indicative of the more open and savanna-like nature of the area in earlier times, include Culver's root and Pennsylvania sedge. The preserve also marks the western-most occurrence of a rare grass known as Nottoway brome. Unknown from Missouri until its discovery at this site, the Accola location is one of only two sites west of the Mississippi River for this rare plant.

But what of the species that are not found at Accola Woods? It seems clear that many of the plants (as well as insects, animals, and invertebrates) that were once part of these woods are gone. According to the 1820 original land survey of the area, open "rich, rolling prairie" extended to within 600 feet of the preserve along its entire western boundary. The woods were described as "broken timber oak and hickory." For the area including Accola Woods, the average distance to a witness tree was fifty-four feet. This gives some impression of the former open nature of the woodlands. Conservancy management activities at the site are designed to test the feasibility of restoring the area to more closely resemble its pre-settlement character, including the use of fire in restoration of the landscape.

Accola Woods is a small preserve and easily accessible to visitors. The north edge of the tract is bordered by a gravel road that becomes quite muddy and difficult to travel in the wetter months. The west and south boundaries of the woods abut pasture and are marked by a barbed wire fence, as is the east boundary line. Access to the preserve is best through the small clearing in the northwest corner of the site. From there one can explore the uplands which are comprised mostly of swamp white oak, shagbark hickory, and bitternut hickory. In the shallow valley running through the preserve, these uplands give way to bottomland woods with elm, cottonwood, silver maple, and swamp white oak. The bottoms are wet and cluttered with leaf litter.

The topography at Accola Woods is gentle, with slight changes in slope and aspect that produce notable changes in the vegetation. Explore the small north-south running drainage that bisects the preserve as well as the slopes and bottomlands that are associated with it. An early spring or autumn walk may prove to be the most enjoyable. In the summer the woods are brushy and the mosquitoes are very hungry. A leisurely walk through the preserve can take anywhere from one to three hours.

ACCOLA WOODS

Lewis County ❧ *40 Acres*

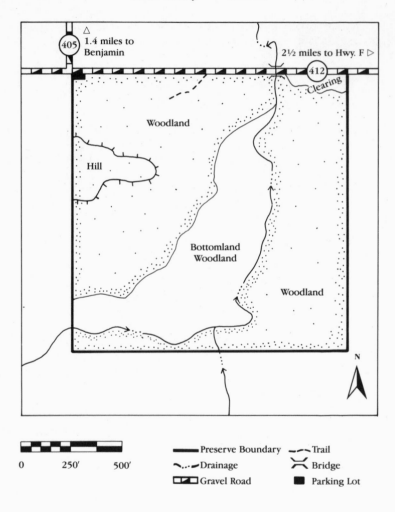

LOCATION
Approximately 1.5 miles north of Highway 16, between Monticello and Canton (Sec. 26, T62N, R7W, Lewis County).

DIRECTIONS
From the junction of Highways 61 and 16 in Canton, proceed west on 16 for approximately 7.5 miles until you come to the junction of Highway Z, on the south side. Turn right (north) on the farm road directly across from Highway Z and follow the road due north 1.75 miles where it curves 90 degrees to the right (east). Continue on one mile until the road forks, with the main fork turning 90 degrees to the left (north). Go straight from the fork (east) for about 50 yards and park on the side of the road. You are now at the northwest corner of the preserve.

USGS
TOPO MAP
Benjamin 7.5 minute quadrangle.

PROTECTED
NATURAL
FEATURES
Natural Community: *Swamp white oak savanna.*
Species: *Nottoway brome, false hellebore.*

BEST TIME
TO GO
Spring or early fall.

HIKING
CONDITIONS
Relatively easy as topography is gentle.

5

HINKSON VALLEY

Just south of downtown Columbia and the University of Missouri, Hinkson Creek meanders west toward the Missouri River. Within the city limits, spanning a loop in the creek, lies the Conservancy's fifty-acre Hinkson Valley preserve.

The Nature Conservancy acquired Hinkson Valley in 1970. It was a gift from landowners who hoped to see the area permanently protected. Although most of the preserve shows considerable past disturbance, from logging, brush clearing, off-road vehicle use, and trash dumping, three distinct natural communities occur here.

Restricted to the flood plain along Hinkson Creek is a mesic bottomland forest. The area is dominated by tall majestic trees including American elm, hackberry, cottonwood, sycamore, and sugar maple, with Virginia wild rye and wood nettle typical of this area's forest floor.

Up the slope from the creek, and in protected ravines and ravine floors, a mesic limestone forest occurs. Here sugar maple, dwarf chinquapin oak, and pawpaw dominate the forest canopy and subcanopy, with bladdernut, jewelweed, wild ginger, and Virginia spiderwort growing underneath.

Above this forest on the upper valley slopes and other well-drained upland sites is a dry-mesic limestone forest. The change between the dry-mesic and mesic limestone forest is gradual. On these drier sites, white oak and black hickory occur with the sugar maples. Here one finds wild leek, recorded in seventeen Missouri counties, but still a plant that is infrequently seen.

Hinkson Valley is an important Columbia metropolitan green-belt area, and provides a pleasant area to spend a few hours.

Hinkson Valley

HINKSON VALLEY

Boone County 🦊 *42.93 Acres*

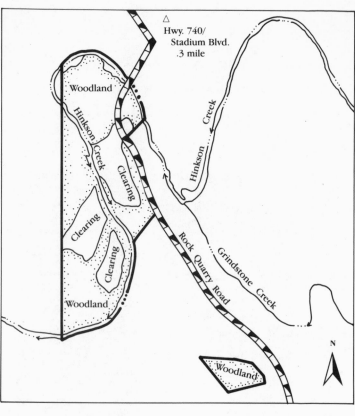

LOCATION

Almost due south of downtown Columbia, Missouri, within the Columbia city limits (Sec. 19, T48N, R12W Boone County).

DIRECTIONS

From I-70, go south on U.S. 63 to the first major intersection (Business Loop 70). Left (east) on Business Loop 70 three blocks to College Avenue (Highway 763). Right (south) on College Avenue (Highway 763). At the intersection with Highway 740, (Stadium Blvd.), go straight onto Rock Quarry Road. After about 0.3 miles, the road crosses a small bridge over Hinkson Creek. Park along the road after crossing the bridge. The preserve is west of the road.

USGS
TOPO MAP

Columbia 7.5 minute quadrangle.

PROTECTED
NATURAL
FEATURES

Natural Communities: *Mesic bottomland forest, mesic limestone forest, dry-mesic limestone forest.* **Species**: *Dwarf chinkapin oak, Virginia wild rye, wild ginger, wild leek.*

BEST TIME
TO GO

All seasons are nice.

HIKING
CONDITIONS

Hilly terrain. A compass is helpful once you are in the preserve.

GLADES

Glades are a unique feature of Missouri's landscape, often sharply contrasting with the surrounding vegetation. Glades are open rocky areas with extensive bedrock at or very close to the surface. Soil cover on glades is thin or absent. These features, plus the fact that many glades are located in sites with southern or western exposures, give rise to extremely harsh, dry conditions for much of the growing season. This same lack of soil and underlying bedrock also causes glades to be saturated and wet through much of the dormant season, with frequent frost heaving and freeze/thaw cycles disrupting the soil pockets.

This combination of extreme conditions creates an environment favoring the survival of specially adapted plants and animals. Glades are largely treeless as a result of the dry summer conditions, thin soils, and frequent wildfires in pre-settlement times. The open, bare rock expanses and thin soils of most glades are characterized by a diverse group of plants, many of which occur nowhere else in the state.

Many glade plants display adaptations for survival in the glade environment, such as the succulent, water-retaining prickly pear cactus, widow's cross, or flower of an hour. Other adaptations include thick, waxy coatings or dense layers of white hairs on leaves to retard water loss, large underground root systems to store water, or tiny, reduced leaf systems to minimize evaporation through transpiration. Many glade plants are winter annuals.

Animals living on glades must also adapt to survive in the sun baked sites, where temperatures of surface rocks can exceed 160 degrees on a summer day. Many glade animals, such as scorpions, tarantulas, and roadrunners, have strong affinities to the dry environments of desert ecosystems. Smaller animals such as insects and spiders often spend the hottest portions of the day underground, emerging only in the cool of night. Others, such as the snakes and lizards, select sites in shade or sun as necessary to maintain their body temperatures. The collared lizard, or "mountain boomer," is the largest and most colorful lizard on Missouri glades. When alarmed, these agile runners sometimes rear up on their hind legs and run like miniature dinosaurs. Some Missouri glades harbor lichen grasshoppers, insects whose mottled coloration perfectly resembles the lichen and rock exposures

Glades

they inhabit. Bachman's sparrow and painted buntings are two rare birds associated with Missouri glades.

Missouri has more known glade area than any other state, with over 400,000 acres of glade at the time of settlement. Six types of glades are recognized in Missouri, based on the underlying bedrock; each is characterized by different plants and animals. Sandstone, igneous, and chert glades are all characterized by acidic, impermeable, sterile bedrock. While each glade type has a different vegetation, these three glades are characterized by some common features, including abundant moss and lichen cover. Glades on limestone and dolomite are by far the most common in the state and contain many rare and restricted species. Shale glades represent an anomalous and poorly understood natural community.

Conservancy preserves in Missouri include several high quality glade systems with numerous rare and unusual species. Sandstone glades occur at Corry Flatrocks, Lichen Glade, and LaBarque Hills; limestone glades at Greenfield Glade; igneous glades at Shut-in Mountain Fens; and dolomite glades at Victoria Glade and LaBarque Hills. ❧

Points of Interest

Glades

6

NANCY B. ALTVATER LABARQUE HILLS

Several of the preserves in this guide bear

the name of Nancy B. Altvater. The late Edna Altvater

established a fund in her daughter's memory to buy

and preserve natural areas in Missouri.

Six miles south of Pacific in northwestern

Jefferson County, the Conservancy's LaBarque Hills Preserve

sprawls across 335 hilly acres of the Ozark borderland. For scenic

interest, this is one of the finest Missouri preserves, but be fore-

warned: It is difficult to find (the hike into the site is 1.5 miles

long), and there are no marked trails on the preserve. A compass,

topographic map, and knowledge of their use is essential.

The LaBarque Hills Preserve was purchased by The Nature

Conservancy in 1986 with money from the Nancy B. Altvater Land

Acquisition Fund. It contains the largest known St. Peter's sand-

stone glade, along with several rare plants. There are also three

separate sandstone canyons along intermittent streams, each with

dazzling cliffs, waterfalls, bowls, overhangs, and other geologic

formations. Bring a camera and explore.

The trail into the preserve crosses privately owned land, on

which the Conservancy owns a forty-foot-wide easement. Please respect the private property and stay on the road and the marked trail. It connects the parking area with the northwest corner of the preserve, which is clearly marked by a yellow Conservancy sign and red flagging on a tall oak tree.

Head southeast from this corner to the first intermittent stream, then follow it northeast as it cuts down through sandstone. Just before it crosses the northern boundary of the preserve, a series of bowls have been eroded by flowing water, after which a waterfall tumbles over a shelf and drops fifteen feet. A diverse flora clings to the rock along this stream, ranging from hairy lip ferns and shining clubmoss to prickly pear cactus.

Due east from this stream channel is a second valley, cut by a slightly larger stream. Throughout this valley, growing in the lower wet areas, is the preserve's rarest species, the heart-leaf plantain. The broad, green, heart-shaped leaves make the plant obvious throughout the summer.

Cross over a ridge that rises to the east 350 feet above the valley floor. A third stream flows generally to the east, eventually crossing the preserve's eastern boundary. The lower reaches of this stream open onto the preserve's largest expanse of St. Peter's sandstone glade.

The ground cover of the glade consists largely of grasses and herbs (little bluestem, rushfoil), with lichens, mosses, ferns, and spikemosses on the more exposed, undisturbed bare rock.

From the point where this creek crosses the eastern boundary of the preserve, up the hill to the northwest, several small glades persist on the contact between sandstone and dolomite. Here typical dolomite glade plants like purple coneflower and prairie dock are found, as well as the rare Fremont's leather flower.

The rest of the preserve is upland forest. The area has been logged in the past, and the forest consists of young, even-aged stands of small trees (six to eighteen inches in diameter).

As you explore the glades in the LaBarque Hills Preserve, it becomes obvious that they are being overgrown by cedars and other small trees. Without proper management these glades will disappear as the trees close in, blocking the sunlight. Suppression of naturally occurring fires appears to be the main cause of the overgrowth of trees. The Conservancy would like to introduce prescribed fire to these glades. Unfortunately, the difficulty of transporting water and fire equipment into the preserve makes such management extremely difficult.

To leave, return to the preserve's northwest corner and retrace the trail back to the parking area. A hike visiting all the areas mentioned above will cover five to seven miles and take four to six hours. Although vigorous, the walk rewards the visitor with scenic geologic features and a diverse flora.

NANCY B. ALTVATER LaBARQUE HILLS

Jefferson County 🦫 *335 Acres*

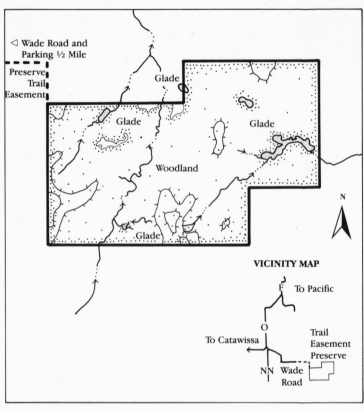

⊲ Wade Road and
Parking ½ Mile

Preserve
Trail
Easement

Glade

Glade

Glade

Woodland

Glade

N

VICINITY MAP

To Pacific

To Catawissa

O

NN Wade
Road

Trail
Easement
Preserve

0   1000'   2000'

▬▬ Preserve Boundary ▬⌒▬ Trail
⌒⋯⌒ Drainage

AT A GLANCE

LOCATION

Approximately six miles south of Pacific, Missouri in northwestern Jefferson County (Sec. 4 and 5, T42N, R3E, Jefferson County).

DIRECTIONS

From Pacific, go south on Highway F 2.5 miles to Highway O. South on Highway O 2.4 miles to Highway NN. South on Highway NN 150 feet, then take an immediate left onto Wade Road (gravel). Follow Wade Road 1.5 miles until it ends at a large metal gate with "Keep Out" and "No Trespassing" signs. On foot, follow the road east past the gate, crossing LaBarque Creek twice. About 100 feet after crossing the creek the second time, pick up the barbwire fence to your left. Follow it across the creek, then head east along the fence across flat ground. (The trail is now marked with blue flagging.) At the base of a steep hill, the trail turns right, up primitive steps, then left over rock outcrops to pick up the fence line at the top of the hill. Continue east along the fence line until the path ends, then turn south (right) and follow the flagging and painted trail markers (a yellow dot over two horizontal lines) to the corner of the preserve. The preserve boundaries are marked, but there are no defined trails within the preserve.

USGS TOPO MAP

Pacific 7.5 minute quadrangle.

PROTECTED NATURAL FEATURES

Natural Communities: *Sandstone cliffs, St. Peter's sandstone glade, dry-mesic forest.*
Species: *Heart-leaf plantain, hairy lip fern, spike moss, lichens, shining clubmoss, Fremont's leather flower.*

**BEST TIME
TO GO**

Winter yields excellent views from the hills; summer, the woods and the rare heart-leaf plantain; spring and fall, the best weather and various flowering plants.

**HIKING
CONDITIONS**

Moderately strenuous up and down the hills.

FREMONT'S LEATHER FLOWER

Scattered through the dolomite glades of east-central Missouri is one of our most enigmatic plants: Fremont's leather flower. A member of the buttercup family, this stately wildflower is in the genus *Clematis*, a name well-known to gardeners for its numerous showy-flowered herbaceous vines. This *Clematis*, however, is not a vine but a low-growing, long-lived perennial adapted to survival in the harsh world of the open glade environment.

Fremont's leather flower occurs only in east-central Missouri, north-central Kansas and a small area of adjacent Nebraska. In both areas the plant grows on glades or dry prairies and slopes with carbonate bedrock.

Fremont's leather flower has large, thick, veiny,

Fremont's Leather Flower

oblong leaves, attached opposite each other along a central stem. The tough leaves are resistant to decay, and the dried and broken stems, with leaves still attached, can often be seen during the winter. Often the thin areas between the veins are eaten by insects or decay, creating a beautiful lace-like dried leaf. The nodding flowers, usually produced in April, are narrowly bell shaped, with thick, petal-like appendages ranging from cream to violet. By midsummer, a round cluster of plumose, long-tailed seeds is produced where each flower was successfully pollinated.

Named for its discoverer, explorer and naturalist John Charles Fremont, little is known about the life cycle of this rare plant. In pioneering work done in Missouri some fifty years ago, including research at what is now Victoria Glade, Ralph Erickson established that the plant is a long-lived perennial with a well-developed underground root system enabling it to survive the rigors of the glade environment. He estimated that it took at least several years for seedlings to develop into mature plants capable of flowering. Little is known about pollination, although the pollen is heavy and probably requires insect transport.

Despite many attempts, scientists have not perfected a method to germinate the seed in cultivation.

In an interesting experiment, Erickson transplanted a number of Fremont's leather flowers to a dolomite glade remote from any wild plants, and monitored their survival. When he revisited the site nearly fifty years later, all but two of the original transplants were thriving, and numerous small offspring dotted the glade. This raises the question of why, if the plant adapts so readily to new glade sites, is it so restricted in its distribution. This becomes all the more perplexing in view of the hundreds of thousands of acres of dolomite glade in Missouri, and the extremely restricted distribution of the leather flower.

While many questions remain unsolved, including much about the life history of the plant, it is known that a high-quality glade environment is necessary for a thriving leather flower population. As we learn more about this plant and the other unique aspects of the glade ecosystem, we can design management techniques aimed at stimulating natural processes, insuring the continued survival of these unique aspects of our natural heritage. ❧

Fremont's Leather Flower

7

VICTORIA GLADE

$\mathbf{B}$arely thirty miles from downtown St. Louis, Victoria Glade seems like another world. Amid the ridge and ravine landscape of this section of the Ozark border, large exposures of shelving dolomite occur on open slopes. During the growing season, the variety and showiness of the vegetation is striking; flowers of all colors and types abound on the glade, including several rare species.

Victoria Glade is unusual in that the large, open glade system occurs on both east- and west-facing slopes bordering a central valley. The Conservancy first began acquisitions in the area in 1979, and today owns about 100 acres along the east side of the Victoria-Hillsboro Road, approximately 2.5 miles south of Hillsboro. An additional 195 acres on the west side of the road was acquired by the Conservancy and later transferred to the Missouri Department of Conservation.

Glades are treeless, rocky barrens with a unique and specially adapted vegetation. Generally found on south- and west- facing slopes, glades are characterized by thin, excessively drained soils and bedrock at or near the ground surface. Although glades occur on numerous rock types, the bedrock at Victoria Glade is composed of dolomite, a type of magnesium-rich limestone.

Glade vegetation consists of a variety of uniquely adapted plants capable of surviving the harsh glade environment. Glade plants and animals must be able to withstand searing summer droughts as well as wet conditions with frequent frost heaving for much of the winter.

Many glade plants are winter annuals that complete their life cycles before the onset of summer droughts; others have dense coats of moisture-conserving hairs or thick, waxy, succulent leaves. Many glade perennials have large root systems to store moisture through the dry periods.

One of the most interesting plants at Victoria Glade is Fremont's leather flower. This long-lived perennial is abundant over much of the open glade. The thick, hairy leaves and nodding, purplish to creamy, vase-shaped flowers make it readily recognizable. Fremont's leather flower occurs only on glades in portions of eastern Missouri and a small area along the Kansas-Nebraska border. Other interesting plants common on the glade include blue wild indigo, American aloe, glade heliotrope, Missouri black-eyed Susan, blazing star, green milkweed, and Indian paintbrush, the latter occurring in both yellow- and red-flowered forms.

The desert-like environment on the glade for much of the growing season creates favorable conditions for many special animals as well. Abundant rocks provide an ideal habitat for scorpions and black widow spiders, as well as numerous snakes and lizards. Several unusual insects occur on the site, including a species of beetle (*Tetraopes texanus*) otherwise known only from the southwestern United States.

All available evidence suggests that the glades in eastern Missouri were open and nearly treeless in presettlement times. In recent years there has been an explosive growth of cedars on glades throughout much of Missouri, including Victoria Glade. The 1817 original land survey for the area makes no mention of cedars, describing the land as "stony, hilly, and poor." Nowhere in the area are there any old-growth cedars. All this information, combined with local accounts of intentional fires in the region through the mid 1960s, suggests that the proliferation of cedars is a recent event due to the decline of fires on the landscape.

A management plan designed to preserve the presettlement character of the glade has been developed. Based upon detailed ecological information about the site, portions of the glade are being burned each spring as part of a comprehensive restoration management program. Ongoing sampling of the vegetation in the management units helps refine the management treatments to ensure the continued protection of this unique ecosystem.

VICTORIA GLADE

Jefferson County ✺ *101 Acres*

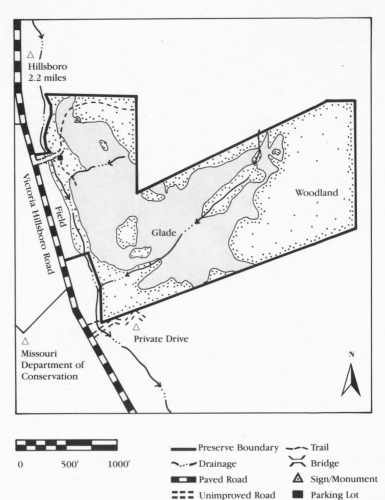

Hillsboro
2.2 miles

Victoria Hillsboro Road

Field

Glade

Woodland

Private Drive

Missouri
Department of
Conservation

N

0	500'	1000'

—— Preserve Boundary ~⌐ Trail
~⋅⌐ Drainage)(Bridge
▰▱ Paved Road △ Sign/Monument
≡≡≡ Unimproved Road ■ Parking Lot

LOCATION	*Approximately 2.5 miles southeast of Hillsboro along Victoria-Hillsboro Road (Sec. 13 and 14, T40N, R4E, Jefferson County).*
DIRECTIONS	*From junction of Highway BB and Highway 21 in Hillsboro, turn east. After several hundred yards the road turns sharply to the right, where it becomes Victoria-Hillsboro Road. Victoria Glade is approximately 2.3 miles from this point on Victoria-Hillsboro Road. Turn left into a small drive that crosses the creek and leads to a parking area (about 100 feet off the road).*
USGS TOPO MAP	*DeSoto 7.5 minute quadrangle.*
PROTECTED NATURAL FEATURES	**Natural Community:** *Dolomite glade.* **Species:** *Fremont's leather flower, blue wild indigo, American aloe, glade heliotrope, Missouri black-eyed Susan, blue gentian, blazing star, green milkweed, Indian paintbrush, plains scorpion, black widow spider.*
BEST TIME TO GO	*Spring, when the most plants are flowering, or fall.*
HIKING CONDITIONS	*Moderately difficult; the glade lies astride a hill, and the surface is rocky.*

◆ 8

SILAS DEES AZALEA
AND WILDFLOWER PRESERVE

A spring visit to Dees Azalea and Wildflower
Preserve enchants the visitor with one of the more beautiful
spring-flowering plants of the Ozarks: the azalea. Blooming among
flowering dogwoods across a steeply sloping hillside, the azaleas
provide a scenic view on this unassuming site.

The Dees Azalea Preserve is a five-acre, hillside tract in
St. Francois County. The area was donated to The Nature Conservancy in January 1967 by Silas and Mabel Dees and is located on the
east side of Highway 00 some ten miles southeast of Farmington.

A prominent wooden sign on the east side of Highway 00
marks the entrance to Dees Preserve. Park along the east side of
the highway, near the sign. The preserve is fenced on all sides, but
adjacent to the sign a gap in the fence allows access to the site.

The entrance opens into the southern end of the preserve, a
flat, forested floodplain. The overstory here, as throughout the
sanctuary, is mostly oak. Part of the headwaters of Little Rock
Creek (a tributary of the Little St. Francis River) runs along the base
of a steep hillside underlain by chert and dolomite of the Derby-
Doerun formation. The azaleas are found on the upper portions
of this slope in the dry, more acidic (cherty) soil, along with

dogwood and other spring-flowering trees and shrubs.

Two distinct natural communities occur at Dees Azalea and Wildflower Preserve, a xeric chert forest on the hillside and a dry to dry-mesic forest at the base of the hill and on the floodplain. The greater soil moisture of the dry-mesic forest supports an over-story of oaks (white, red, black, and post), with plants like paw paw, Arkansas bedstraw, black cohosh, wild ginger, and rattle-snake and bracken ferns beneath.

The drier, cherty hillside overstory harbors red maples and blackjack oak along with the same oaks as occur in the floodplain. A slightly different group of plants is found underneath. In addi-tion to the azaleas and dogwoods, understory plants growing in the thin, dry soil of the hillside include lowbush blueberry, dit-tany, goat's rue, and ebony spleenwort.

No rare animals are known from the site. The usual woodland mammal species may be found here (Eastern cottontail rabbit, deer, raccoon, opossum), along with woodland birds like the pileated woodpecker and reptiles that include the fence lizard, three-toed turtle, and several species of snakes.

Dees Azalea and Wildflower Preserve is well-known in the greater Farmington region for nature appreciation and outdoor education. The oak woodland found here is typical of this part of the Ozarks. There are no developed trails, but the understory

is relatively open and easy to walk through, even in summer. Its
small size makes the site easy to explore in an hour or so.

Although spring is perhaps the most beautiful time to visit,
a stop in any season will be rewarding. Silas Dees Azalea and
Wildflower Preserve is a small piece of Missouri's Ozark
natural heritage where beauty can be enjoyed year round.

SILAS DEES AZALEA AND WILDFLOWER PRESERVE

Saint Francois County ❧ *5 Acres*

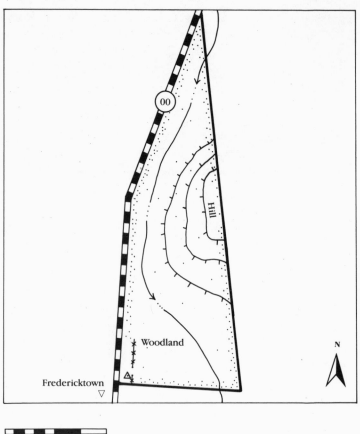

00

Hill

Woodland

Fredericktown

N

0	150′	300′

Preserve Boundary ✻✻✻ Fence

⟍⋯⟋ Drainage ✻•✻ Fence Gap

▰▱▰ Paved Road △ Sign/Monument

LOCATION
On the east side of State Route 00, 1.75 miles north of the Saint Francois County/Madison County line (Sec. 8, T34N, R7E, Saint Francois County).

DIRECTIONS
From the junction of Highway 32 and State Route 00 just east of Farmington, proceed south on Highway 00 for approximately eleven miles. A sign on the east side of the road marks the preserve.

**USGS
TOPO MAP**
Knob Lick 7.5 minute quadrangle.

**PROTECTED
NATURAL
FEATURES**
Natural Community: *Xeric chert forest, dry to dry-mesic forest.*
Species: *Azalea, black cohosh, Arkansas bedstraw.*

**BEST TIME
TO GO**
Spring for the showy azaleas and dogwoods. Fall colors are also beautiful.

**HIKING
CONDITIONS**
Easy in the flat lowland, but the steeply-sloping hillside is strenuous to climb.

9

NANCY B. ALTVATER GRASSHOPPER HOLLOW

In a narrow, green Ozark valley in Reynolds County, at least fifteen fens of various types can be found—the largest and most significant fen complex in unglaciated North America. The Conservancy's preserve at Grasshopper Hollow, the north/south valley that is the site of these fens, protects five rare plants and two rare animals.

The Grasshopper Hollow area has been disturbed over the last century by logging and grazing. Still, the fens have managed to survive. These freshwater wetlands are formed by water percolating through the dolomite bedrock of the surrounding hills and coming to the surface in the valley floor. This constant supply of mineral-rich groundwater supports unique plant life.

The first view a visitor gets of the site exemplifies the disturbance that has occurred in the past: just past the gate is a large clearing with the remains of an old sawmill. Follow the road across this sawmill and along the western hillside for another quarter mile. As you walk along, glimpses of alder and willow thickets to the right mark a fen. Farther along, these thickets diminish and the open fen is visible through the trees.

At the end of this road, an old house sits on a hill. The fens become open to view here. To the south, a fen stands on wet, stony ground, with knee-deep standing water in some areas. The fen is laced with beaver runs among the grasses and sedges. Many less-conspicuous plants, such as swamp agrimony and arrowleaved tear-thumb, grow among them. Be careful in all the fens: cordgrass and the abundant rice cut-grass can scratch the skin. Willow and alder thickets inhibit travel to the south.

North, past a large beaver impoundment near the house and a man-made pond, is a prairie fen, the largest known in Missouri. In late summer and early fall, prairie cordgrass, big bluestem, and Indian grass are lush. New England aster, rough-leaf goldenrod, and Michigan lily also decorate the land.

Further north, more fens can be found. Fortunate visitors may spot one of the five rare plants or two rare animals known to exist in the valley: heart-leaf plantain, wild sweet William, tussock sedge, marsh bellflower, marsh blue violet, the four-toed salaman-der, and the wood frog. Other fen plants include marsh fern, grass of parnassus, swamp goldenrod, swamp thistle, and leafy bulrush.

The hills on either side of Grasshopper Hollow are mostly owned by the U.S. Forest Service, and are densely forested, mostly in hardwood. The region was initially surveyed during May through July 1821, and the surveyor's notes indicate an open and essentially pine-dominated region. The hillsides here were almost entirely short-leaf pine, with limited amounts of oak.

The hardwoods that now dominate the hillsides may affect the fen community, because they transpire vastly more water than do pines, and thus impact the groundwater reaching the fens. An entire 1,600-acre area within Grasshopper Hollow is being protected by The Nature Conservancy, U.S. Forest Service, Doe Run Company, and Missouri Department of Conservation through a unique joint management agreement. Under this plan, scientists are working to restore the area to its pre-settlement condition.

Visitors to Grasshopper Hollow have the privilege of viewing one of the rarest natural communities in Missouri. A fall visit, when the leaves change, is perhaps the most spectacular, but any season reveals interesting aspects of this preserve.

Nancy B. Altvater Grasshopper Hollow

NANCY B. ALTVATER GRASSHOPPER HOLLOW

Reynolds County 🐸 120 Acres

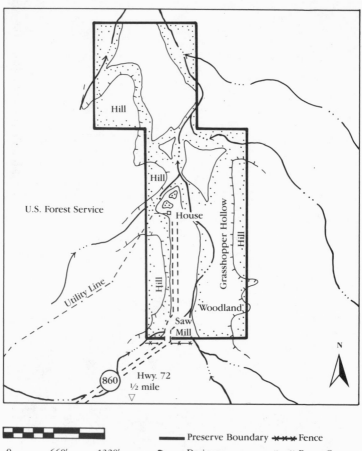

U.S. Forest Service

Hill

Hill

Hill

Hill

House

Grasshopper Hollow

Woodland

Saw Mill

Utility Line

Hwy. 72
½ mile

860

N

0 660' 1320'	

━━━ Preserve Boundary ✳✳✳ Fence
〜··〜 Drainage ✳• •✳ Fence Gap
▀▀▀ Unimproved Road

LOCATION	*About one-half mile north of Highway 72, approximately one mile west of Highway B and one mile east of Highway TT (Sec. 31, T32N, R1W, Reynolds County).*
DIRECTIONS	*From Centerville in Reynolds County, go south on Highway 21 to Highway 72. Take Highway 72 west to its junction with Highway B; continue west about a mile. Turn right onto County Road 860. Parking for one or two vehicles is available on a cleared spot immediately to the left. The preserve is reached by a half mile hike up the road, passing a gate with a Nature Conservancy posting, an old sawmill, and finally an abandoned house at the end of the road. The preserve here is marked with a wooden sign.*
USGS TOPO MAP	*Corridon 7.5 minute quadrangle.*
PROTECTED NATURAL FEATURES	**Natural Community:** *Fen, Prairie Fen, Deep Muck Fen.* **Species:** *Heart-leaf plantain, wild sweet William, tussock sedge, marsh bellflower, marsh blue violet, four-toed salamander, wood frog.*
BEST TIME TO GO	*Summer or early fall highlights the lush grasses and sedges and many showy flowers.*
HIKING CONDITIONS	*The fens are on level or gently sloping ground, but deep standing water makes for mucky ground. Wear waterproof boots and long pants. In summer, deer flies can be bothersome.*

GRAY BAT

Gray bats are small, nocturnal, flying mammals.
They generally have dark grayish-brown fur, although
some can be russet in color. They spend most of the
daylight hours in shelter, leaving their caves in the
evening and returning at dawn.

Most bats feed for an hour or two at twilight, and
again just before sunrise. Some forage periodically
throughout the night. Their diet varies depending
upon the types of flying insects that are available
throughout the warmer months.

Of the fourteen bat species that are found in
Missouri, the gray bat is the only one that lives in
caves throughout the year. Most hibernate in only
three caves located in southern Missouri. Each spring,
they disperse northward to smaller, warmer caves,
preferably near reservoirs, rivers, or streams that have
abundant food. Females generally occupy caves
separate from males and yearlings. In these maternity
caves, females give birth to a single young. The gray
bat is listed on both the state and federal endangered
species lists. Although gray bat numbers seem to have
stabilized during the last ten years, they are at levels
about twenty-five percent lower than they used to be.

Points of Interest

Human activities are the greatest threats to cave-dwelling bats. Cave disturbance by spelunkers or commercialization can cause bats to desert the cave, females to abort young, young bats to fall to the cave floor, or hibernating bats to awake and use stored energy necessary for their winter survival. When streams are channelized and forests are mismanaged, feeding areas are lost. Reservoirs can flood caves and improper installation of gates to protect bat caves can actually eliminate their use by the bats. To ensure this species continues to exist, protection of important hibernation and maternity caves is necessary. 🦇

Gray Bat

10

LILY POND

After hiking for nearly a mile through oak-pine forests on the rugged, rocky slopes typical of the Ozarks, Lily Pond appears as an anomaly on the landscape. Here, in a dry, rocky upland, lies a small depression with dense, luxuriant vegetation and standing water. Although small and difficult to get to, Lily Pond is an important window to a long-lost phase in the development of the Ozarks. The preserve was donated to the Conservancy by John and Anita Marsland in 1961.

Some fifty million years ago, the Ozark region of Missouri was a low-lying, swampy region, with vast woodlands, resembling in many aspects portions of the Missouri bootheel. When this area was uplifted, then subjected to millions of years of erosion, the present day Ozarks were formed. In the process, the swamp forests and wetland vegetation were replaced with upland vegetation.

Remnants of the original lowland vegetation from past ages continue to survive in a few special zones, known as sink-hole ponds. These ponds, formed in ancient carbonate rocks when cave systems collapse, retain conditions that have allowed the survival of plant species for millions of years.

The dense, almost impenetrable, vegetation choking Lily Pond contains numerous special plants that in Missouri are usually found only in sink-hole ponds, including swamp rose and Walter's St. John's wort. Lush mats of sphagnum moss are common in the pond. Endangered species occurring at the site include swamp loosestrife, water violet, and the rare epiphytic sedge. The latter plant almost always grows on the bases of buttonbush plants. Water violet, not a true violet at all, is a bizarre-looking plant with inflated basal portions, allowing it to float free on the water surface. Additionally, two other rare plants, ribbon-leaved pondweed and Engelmann's quillwort, are known historically from the pond, but have not been seen in recent times.

Lily Pond is managed by the Missouri Department of Conservation and is a State Natural Area.

Lily Pond

LILY POND

Reynolds County 🏕 *8.23 Acres*

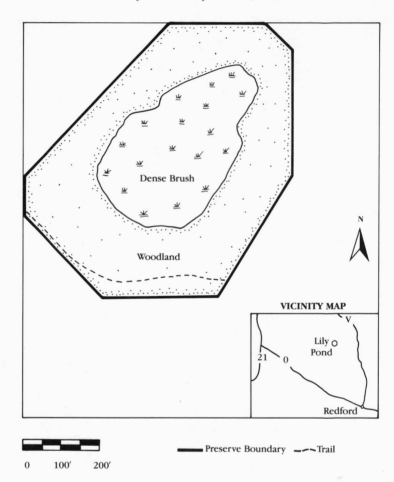

Dense Brush

Woodland

N

VICINITY MAP

V

Lily Pond

21   0

Redford

0   100'   200'

━━ Preserve Boundary   ━╴╴ Trail

AT A GLANCE

LOCATION

Approximately five miles southeast of Centerville (Sec.23, T31N, R1E, Reynolds County).

DIRECTIONS

Access to this site is by permission only. Lily Pond is difficult to locate and requires crossing private land. It is located nearly a mile from the nearest road. For directions contact the Missouri Field Office at 2800 S. Brentwood, St. Louis, Missouri, 63144, (314) 968-1105.

USGS TOPO MAP

Redford 7.5 minute quadrangle.

PROTECTED NATURAL FEATURES

Natural Community: *Sinkhole Pond (Pond Shrub Swamp).*
Species: *Swamp loosestrife, water violet, epiphytic sedge, swamp rose, Walter's St. John's wort. Historic site for Engelmann's quillwort and ribbon-leaved pondweed.*

BEST TIME TO GO

Midsummer, when swamp loosestrife cloaks the shrub mat in the pond with magenta.

HIKING CONDITIONS

Walking to the pond is long and steep. Familiarity with map and compass is requisite. The pond itself is sensitive to disturbance and difficult to walk through. Please stay along the margins.

11

NANCY B. ALTVATER PONDBERRY PRESERVE

Just a few yards from the Arkansas border in southeastern Missouri, the land takes on a different character from the rugged Ozark highlands just to the north. The topography is essentially flat, with slight undulations. Farm fields have cotton and rice, further testimony to the southern affinities of this region. Here, one of America's rarest shrubs is preserved at the 105-acre Nancy B. Altvater Pondberry Preserve.

This area is unique for Missouri: it is the only region of sand dunes in the state. These low dunes, the result of ancient, wind-deposited sands, create a gentle swell and swale landscape that is inhabited by a unique community. For much of the winter and spring, the interdunal depressions and much of the uplands are underwater. As the growing season progresses, water levels drop until water remains only in the low depressions, and in late summer of dry years, most depressions eventually dry out. By early fall, water levels begin to rise, and the cycle begins anew.

This specialized water cycle, unique substrate, and southern climatic influence of the Mississippi basin, all combine to create conditions favorable to a natural community found nowhere else in the Midwest. The preserve was originally wooded, although portions of it are now actively farmed. These woodlands are a rich mix of bald cypress, water oak, swamp white oak, Nuttall's oak, willow oak, red maple, sweet gum, black gum, pumpkin ash, and swamp cottonwood. Here, in low depressions that remain wet to moist through most of the year, are dense stands of pondberry—a low shrub with simple leaves, aromatic foliage, and bright red fruits. Known only from a very few widely scattered sites in the southeastern United States, pondberry is closely related to the more common spicebush, which occurs on the upland portions of the preserve. Pondberry produces small, light yellow flowers in early spring, before the leaves have emerged.

In addition to pondberry, several other special plants occur at the site. One is *Carex abscondita*, a sedge that has no common name. Only recently discovered in Missouri, this southern sedge occurs nowhere else in the state. Other typical plants—all characteristic of southeastern swampy environments—include copper iris, climbing dogbane, snowbell, yellow leafcup, lady's eardrops, and Virginia willow. Other plants on the site include pipe-vine, strawberry bush, partridge berry, and broad beech fern.

Little is known about animals inhabiting the site, although there is a breeding population of green tree frogs, a species with a limited distribution in Missouri. Although often difficult to explore, a trip to this site provides a glimpse of the humid, lush southeastern component of Missouri's natural heritage.

Nancy B. Altvater Pondberry Preserve

NANCY B. ALTVATER PONDBERRY PRESERVE

Ripley County ❧ *105 Acres*

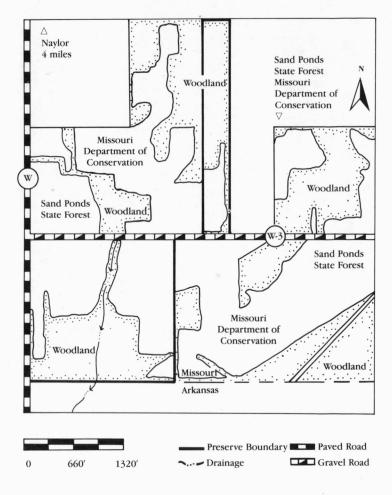

Naylor
4 miles

Woodland

Sand Ponds
State Forest
Missouri
Department of
Conservation

N

Missouri
Department of
Conservation

W

Woodland

Sand Ponds
State Forest

Woodland

W-3

Sand Ponds
State Forest

Woodland

Missouri
Department of
Conservation

Woodland

Missouri

Arkansas

| 0 | 660' | 1320' |

— Preserve Boundary ▰▰ Paved Road
∿‥⌣ Drainage ◩◩ Gravel Road

LOCATION | *On the Arkansas state line, approximately 3.5 miles south of Naylor (Sec. 35, T22N, R4E, Ripley County).*

DIRECTIONS | *From Naylor, go south on Highway W for approximately 2.5 miles to the junction with Highway AA; continue south on W for another 1.0 mile, then turn east (left) onto a small dirt road. Proceed 0.4 miles to a sign for Sand Ponds State Forest, park here. The best pondberry viewing is in the wooded depressions to the northeast.*

USGS TOPO MAP | *Naylor 7.5 minute quadrangle.*

PROTECTED NATURAL FEATURES | **Natural Community:** *Sand ponds forest (a special type of wet bottomland forest).*
Species: *Pondberry, Nuttall's oak, Carex abscondita, slender spike grass, savanna sedge, Virginia willow, water oak, green tree frog.*

BEST TIME TO GO | *Late summer to early fall, when pondberry fruits are developed and water levels lower. Early spring visitors who don't mind wading will be rewarded with sights of flowering pondberries.*

HIKING CONDITIONS | *Portions of the site may be wet any time, with fairly deep (3-4 feet) water zones possible. Insects can be a problem, and there are numerous zones of spiny vines and shrubs.*

Note on the map, the Missouri Department of Conservation Sand Ponds State Forest is adjacent to the preserve. This area includes similar lands with pondberry.

Original Missouri Land Survey Notes

B*ecause so little information was recorded* about the undisturbed landscape of Missouri by those who knew it firsthand, the few written documents we have are precious. The field notes of the original public land survey contain the most comprehensive and accurate records and descriptions of Missouri's pre-settlement landscape.

The Missouri surveys began in 1815, and most of the state was completed by the 1850s. Professional surveyors, hired by the federal government, subcontracted for the rest of their crew (brush cutters, chain-men, axe-men, and flag-men), each of whom was required to take an oath swearing to fulfil their duties with the utmost accuracy. The surveys themselves were governed by a systematic plan with detailed procedural instructions. The notes portray the land and vegetation in a regular grid system of lines and points that cover the entire state.

Missouri is divided into a series of squares six miles on each side, called townships. Each township is then subdivided into thirty-six one-mile-square sections. Early land surveyors walked the section boundaries and marked each section corner. (To this

Points of Interest

day, these corners are the basis of all real property in Missouri, and are the required starting point of all land surveys admitted as evidence in court.)

As they measured and marked the section lines, the surveyors were required to record certain features of the land they were surveying. These features were to be noted along section lines and at section corners. They included two or four witness trees at each corner, to identify the exact location of the corner, any trees that occurred on the section line, major topographic features, any water features, the natural communities present (i.e., timber, prairie, barrens) and the points along the section line where the natural community types changed, and any other unusual natural features.

Witness trees had to be identified by common name, and the diameter, bearing, and distance from the corner had to be indicated. Trees occurring on a section line had to be identified by common name, and the diameter and distance from the section corner recorded. These, combined with the descriptions of the natural communities present, can be used to construct a relatively detailed picture of early Missouri prior to the arrival of settlers.

Original Missouri Land Survey Notes

An example of the detail recorded in these notes can be seen in the April 1819 survey of the area around the Conservancy's Trice-Dedman Preserve. Descriptions are along section lines (original spelling included):

"Land good soil, gentel roling. Timber oak hickery (line between sec 18 and 19) . . . Gentel roling timber, oak, walnut hickery. Undergroath hazel and vines. 36″ white oak, 20″ black walnut, 18″ black walnut, 40″ black oak (line between sec. 19 and 20) . . . Land, thin soil, roling. Timber oak, hickory, mostly prairie. 24″ white oak, 12″ black oak (line between sec. 20 and 21)."

Many ecologists believe the records of early land surveyors are the single most reliable source of information on pre-settlement ecological composition. Because they represent a reasonably standardized, systematic sample of the vegetation, survey records can be statistically compared with each other and to samples from modern vegetation.

The Nature Conservancy uses land survey notes in several ways: to identify and map plant commun-ities and species distribution prior to European settlement; to compare the pre-settlement condition to the present, usually altered one; and to provide guidelines for natural area inventory and management.

The surveys are also used by Conservancy scientists to provide baseline ecological data for each of our preserves. Many times, the surveys indicate a much different pre-settlement ecosystem than currently occurs, and a key part of our challenge to protect these areas for our children and grandchildren involves understanding the reason for such compositional changes. ❧

Original Missouri Land Survey Notes

12

NANCY B. ALTVATER SHUT-IN MOUNTAIN FENS

Shut-In Mountain Fens is an area of grand vistas and spectacular scenery. Located along Wildcat Hollow in Shannon County, southeast of Eminence, this 520-acre preserve contains a representative spectrum of St. Francois Mountain landscape features and natural communities.

The preserve was acquired in 1988 from Mrs. Evelyne Bolin and her daughter, Mrs. Tru Loy. The land had been in their family for several generations, and through their cooperation and desire to see the area permanently preserved, The Nature Conservancy was able to protect the site. Shut-In Mountain was named for a shut-in, or constriction of a stream into a narrow rocky gorge, that occurs along Little Rocky Creek north of the preserve.

The preserve itself is named for its two most significant features—a series of three small fen communities along Wildcat Hollow, and Shut-In Mountain, a rugged red rhyolite dome rising 350 feet above the adjacent valley. These features represent two extremes of moisture, elevation, acidity, and nutrient availability, which provide habitat for a diversity of plants and animals.

Fens are special wetlands characterized by a constant supply of mineralized groundwater seeping to the surface, which creates a unique environment favorable to various types of rare plants.

The three small fens at Shut-In Mountain contain several characteristic fen plants, including the small fruited false loosestrife, a low herb with greenish yellow flowers, and tussock sedge, a tall, grasslike plant. Each fen offers a unique opportunity for exploration. One is a large, wet, gravelly expanse with scattered low sedges and grass pink orchids. Another is an intricate mixture of glade-like rock outcrops and small seepage zones, and the third is an expanse of tall sedges and wildflowers on a saturated mat of quaking muck.

A short (but largely uphill) hike from the fens is Shut-In Mountain itself, an ancient knob of hard, red, granite-like rock called rhyolite. The lower, moderately sloping flanks of the mountain become steeper and more encrusted with boulders and talus as one ascends. The sparsely timbered woodlands on the dry sterile upper slopes contain a mixture of black oak, blackjack oak, and black hickory. This area, termed xeric igneous forest, is a high-quality example of this natural community type. The summit of Shut-In Mountain is a mixture of open igneous glade and gnarled stunted trees clinging to crevices in the exposed rock. The view from here is spectacular—a breathtaking vista for miles in all directions that makes the effort of the climb worthwhile.

Elsewhere on the preserve are scenic streambeds with rock outcrops and ledges harboring a number of unusual plants, and wooded slopes with a rich complement of ferns and wildflowers.

Late spring and early fall are among the more rewarding times to explore Shut-In Mountain Fens. The area is open to the public for hiking and nature study, although we ask that visitors do not walk in the fens themselves (which would mean wet feet anyway).

GRASS PINK ORCHID
A handsome, pink-flowered orchid that occurs in a few fens and wet areas in prairies.

NANCY B. ALTVATER SHUT-IN MOUNTAIN FENS

Shannon County 🐾 *520 Acres*

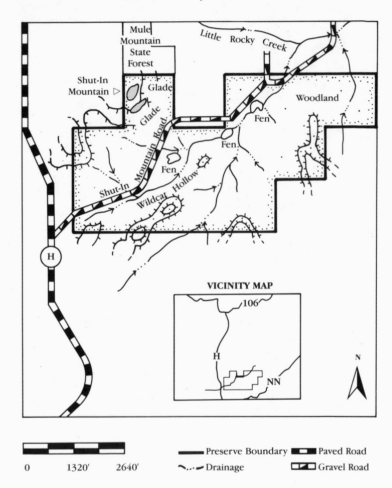

Mule Mountain State Forest

Little Rocky Creek

Shut-In Mountain ▷

Glade

Glade

Woodland

Fen

Fen

Shut-In Mountain Road

Fen

Shut-In Wildcat Hollow

H

VICINITY MAP

106

H

NN

N

0   1320'   2640'

—— Preserve Boundary   ▮▮ Paved Road
◠⋯◡ Drainage   ▭◪◩ Gravel Road

AT A GLANCE

LOCATION

Approximately 2.5 miles south of Highway 106 east of Eminence (Sec. 11 and 12, T28N, R3W, Shannon County, Missouri).

DIRECTIONS

From Eminence, in central Shannon County, take Highway 106 east 6.5 miles. Turn right (south) on Highway H and proceed 2.0 miles to Shut-In Mountain Road. Turn left (east) on Shut-In Mountain Road and go 0.5 miles. Park along the side of the road; the preserve is on both sides of the road.

USGS
TOPO MAP

Stegall Mountain 7.5 minute quadrangle.

PROTECTED
NATURAL
ELEMENTS

Natural Communities: *Fen, Xeric igneous forest.* **Species:** *Bobcat, grass pink orchid, small-fruited false loosestrife.*

BEST TIME
TO GO

Late spring for flowering plants, early fall for fall colors, winter for a clear view from the top of Shut-In Mountain.

HIKING
CONDITIONS

The hiking varies from moderate to strenuous, and ground may be wet in spots in the spring.

13

HYER WOODS

Hyer Woods was donated to the Conservancy in 1959 by Mr. and Mrs. John Bowles as a memorial to the pioneer doctors of the Ozark region. This thirty-acre woodland tract consists primarily of south-facing slopes along a small stream, Hyer Branch. Within this small preserve are two springs, exposed rock outcrops, and a variety of plant and animal life. Hyer Woods is leased to the Missouri Department of Conservation for management.

Although classified today as "upland oak-hickory forest," data from the 1823 land survey reveal that the site was once an open savanna-like landscape with scattered trees. Twenty-one trees were recorded as witness points in the section containing Hyer Woods; nine of these were blackjack oaks and twelve were post oaks; no other trees were even mentioned for the area. The average distance to a witness tree was more than ninety-three feet— such distances imply an open, sparsely timbered landscape. Comments made in the surveyor's journal for the section include "land hilly poor barrens timber oak" and "land poor brushy barrens timber thin post oak and black jack."

Despite the changes that have occurred at Hyer Woods since settlement, natural indicators of the quality of the site are still discernable. On the upper slopes, a few large, old black and post oaks hold their own. The growth form of these trees is what foresters call "open grown"—large branches spreading horizontally starting low on the trunk. Such a growth form implies that the tree was established in an open landscape, and did not have to compete with surrounding tall vegetation for light. On the older trees at Hyer Woods, the lower branches have been shade pruned as the surrounding woodland has become overgrown, but the original growth form of these "old soldiers" is still evident.

Because the site includes a variety of habitats, ranging from streamside wetlands and springs to dry rocky uplands, Hyer Woods contains an unusually rich diversity of plant life for such a small site. Trees at the site include black, white, shingle, chinquapin, post, and red oak, as well as blackgum, elm, and white ash. Flowering dogwood, hawthorn, serviceberry, black haw, hazelnut, and buckbrush are common in the understory. Moister sites also have shrubs like bladdernut and river birch.

Rock outcrops on the slope harbor several ferns, including ebony spleenwort, rattlesnake fern, bulbet fern, hairy lip fern, purple cliff brake, and rusty woodsia. A few of the numerous other plants of interest at the site include Virginia snakeroot, rattlesnake master, sensitive briar, goat's rue, horse gentian, and Culver's root.

This small preserve can be seen in a relatively short time, and its easy access makes it a desirable stop for travelers who wish to experience a quick vignette of a remnant Ozark woodland. Traces of an old road run through the tract just above the stream, making for an enjoyable, relaxing walk.

HYER WOODS

Dent County 🐾 *30 Acres*

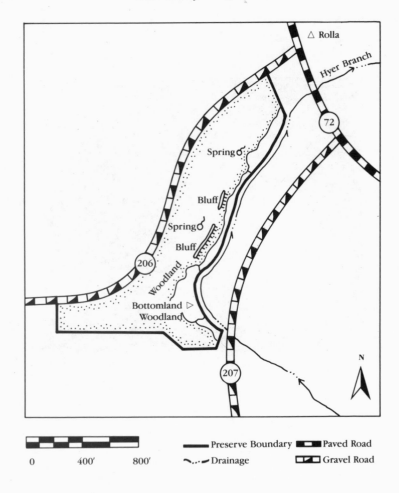

0   400'   800'

Preserve Boundary   Paved Road
Drainage   Gravel Road

AT A GLANCE

LOCATION

Approximately fifteen miles south of Rolla, just west of Highway 72, near the small community of Lake Spring (Sec. 3, T35N, R7W, Dent County).

DIRECTIONS

From Rolla, proceed south on Highway 72 for approximately fifteen miles, turn west (right) onto a small gravel road, and proceed for about a quarter mile to the metal sign along the road. The preserve is situated on the slope below the road, running down to the stream. From the south, proceed north on Highway 72 approximately 2.5 miles from the junction with Highway F, taking the first gravel road west (left) after crossing the bridge over Hyer Branch.

USGS TOPO MAP

Lecoma 7.5 minute quadrangle.

PROTECTED NATURAL FEATURES

Natural Community: *Old growth upland forest.*
Species: *Ferns, wildflowers, variety of trees and shrubs.*

BEST TIME TO GO

Late spring from May to early June for wildflowers, fall for colorful foliage.

HIKING CONDITIONS

Some parts of the site are steep and rocky.

14

ZAHORSKY WOODS

Located on the Meramec River just north of Steelville, Zahorsky Woods is an ideal place for a nature hike in spring, summer, or fall. This fifty-six acre woodland is enhanced by a mixture of ridges, ravines, bluffs, and bottomlands with a diversity of natural communities. During even a short visit to this site, one can sample a broad range of interesting topographic features that characterize the Upper Ozark Region.

Zahorsky Woods Nature Preserve was given to the Conservancy in 1974 by Elizabeth and Joseph Cushing in memory of Mrs. Cushing's parents, Dr. and Mrs. John Zahorsky. A pioneer physician, Dr. Zahorsky practiced pediatrics in the St. Louis area from around the turn of the century until his retirement many years later. A sign honoring the Zahorskys marks the southern corner of the preserve.

Geologically, Zahorsky Woods is part of the Salem Plateau, an ancient uplifted plain that has been carved and dissected by rivers and streams for thousands of years. Here, near the Meramec River, the alluvial soils of the floodplain support a bottomland forest dominated by sycamore and silver maple with clearweed, goldenglow, wood nettle, poison ivy, and Virginia wild rye in the understory. Other portions of the bottomland contain young, closed-canopy stands of box elder and silver maple. The floodplain has an eeriness about it that is enchanting; that is if you don't mind getting your feet wet, for flooding is frequent.

Rising nearly 100 feet above the floodplain in the northeast corner of Zahorsky Woods is a steep dolomite bluff overlooking the river. The loose talus slopes on the sides of the bluff support chinquapin oak, hackberry, and musclewood, but the species composition changes at the top of the bluff. There, interspersed among widely spaced blackjack oaks, are small glades showcasing a variety of glade forbs and grasses such as Missouri black-eyed Susan and side oats grama.

On the steep south- and west-facing slopes of the bluff and nearby ridges, the glade community blends into upland chert forest. Post oak, white oak, and black hickory comprise the overstory on these dry, acidic upland soils. Sun-loving species such as leadplant, purple aster, and dittany can be found in the more open glades. Additional vegetation changes occur on the north and east sides of slopes and in ravine bottoms. Deeper, less-acidic soils in these areas support flowering dogwood, serviceberry, and sugar maple as well as Virginia creeper, bare-stemmed tick trefoil, and large-flowered bellwort. Wild turkeys can be seen frequently sauntering through the woods.

Despite its rugged terrain, Zahorsky Woods is accessible and relatively easy to get around in. There are no interior trails at the site but the boundaries are clearly marked with yellow signs and portions of barbwire fence. A leisurely hike over most of the preserve takes only two to three hours. Note that two private inholdings intersect Conservancy-owned land along Highway 19. Please respect these property lines.

Parking is available along Highway 19, which borders the west side of the property (see the right-of-way access on the map), or at the southern corner of the tract at the intersection of Highway 19 and the county road marked Grand. Zahorsky Woods is only about ninety miles southwest of St. Louis.

As you walk through Zahorsky Woods, try to imagine it as Dr. Zahorsky would have seen it in 1900. If you are fortunate enough to be looking out over the Meramec on an autumn day, think about the processes that have shaped the area over time. As a nature preserve Zahorsky Woods offers a unique glimpse of the ecological history of one of the oldest geologic regions in the world: the Ozarks.

ZAHORSKY WOODS

Crawford County 🐾 *56 Acres*

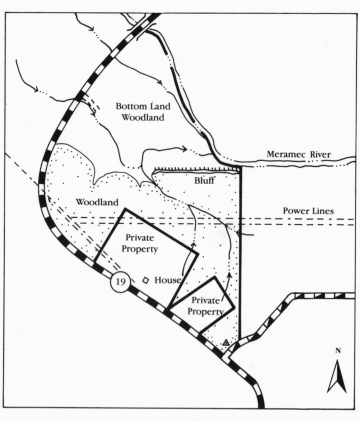

Bottom Land Woodland

Meramec River

Bluff

Woodland

Power Lines

Private Property

19 ◇ House

Private Property

N

0   500'   1000'

━━━ Preserve Boundary ▪▪▪ Unimproved Road
🗲‥‿ Drainage ✕ Bridge
▰▱▰ Paved Road ▲ Sign/Monument
▱▰▱ Gravel Road

LOCATION	*On the east side of Highway 19, one mile north of Steelville between Grand Road and the Meramec River (Sec. 28 & 33, T38N, R4W, Crawford County).*
DIRECTIONS	*From Interstate 44, proceed south on Highway 19 towards Steelville. Go approximately 6.5 miles until you cross the Meramec River. The preserve begins at the south edge of the bridge. Continue on Highway 19 and park along the right-of-way (see map) or at the south end of the property near the sign.*
USGS TOPO MAP	*Steelville 7.5 minute quadrangle.*
PROTECTED NATURAL FEATURES	**Natural Communities:** *Dry upland forest, bottomland forest and glade/savanna.* **Species:** *Clearweed, goldenglow, Virginia wild rye, Missouri blackeyed Susan, side oats grama.*
BEST TIME TO GO	*Spring, summer or fall. Fall colors are especially nice when viewed from the bluff.*
HIKING CONDITIONS	*Relatively easy, but steep slopes are present. Bottomlands can be wet or flooded during spring or fall.*

15

ALMA PETERSON AZALEA MEMORIAL

Alma Peterson Azalea Memorial is a three-acre site donated to the Conservancy in 1961 by Elmer Peterson in memory of his mother. The site allows ready access to a population of azalea, known for its spectacular spring flowers.

The preserve consists largely of degraded upland forests on sandy soils derived from underlying sandstone bedrock. Common canopy trees at the site include shortleaf pine, white oak, black gum, and black hickory. Shrubs and understory trees in addition to the azalea include flowering dogwood, deerberry, and lowbush blueberry. The forest in the northern portion of the tract is of somewhat better quality.

The preserve is especially beautiful in the spring when the azaleas are in flower and, when combined with a stop at the nearby N.L. Williams Memorial Woods, makes for a pleasant outing.

Alma Peterson Azalea Memorial

ALMA PETERSON AZALEA MEMORIAL

Douglas County ❧ *2.6 Acres*

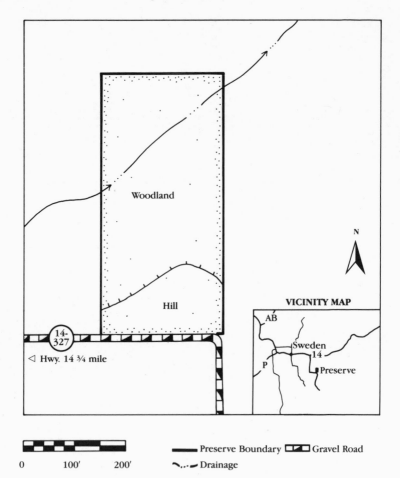

Woodland

Hill

14-327

◁ Hwy. 14 ¾ mile

N

VICINITY MAP

AB

Sweden

14

P

Preserve

—— Preserve Boundary ▨ Gravel Road

0   100'   200'

◥⋯◤ Drainage

AT A GLANCE

LOCATION

Approximately 14 miles southeast of Ava, or about 1.2 miles southeast of the small town of Sweden (Sec. 8, T25N, R14W, Douglas County).

DIRECTIONS

From the junction of Highways P and 14 (approximately 12 miles southeast of Ava), proceed east on Highway 14 for approximately 1.5 miles, and turn south (right) on a gravel road. After about 0.6 miles, this road turns east (left), then continues for approximately 0.3 miles before turning south (right) again. When the road turns south, you are at the south end of the preserve; a stone marker is located here, with an old trail leading north into the site.

USGS
TOPO MAP

Ava 15 minute quadrangle.

PROTECTED
NATURAL
FEATURES

Species: *Azalea.*

BEST TIME
TO GO

The last week of April through mid May.

HIKING
CONDITIONS

Allow about an hour at the site.

16

N. L. WILLIAMS MEMORIAL WOODS

This preserve provides an opportunity to walk through a picturesque narrow valley fed by permanent small spring-seeps draining sandstone-strewn slopes. Although signs of previous logging activity can be seen, the timbered slopes provide many scenic vistas. The preserve was donated to the Conservancy in 1975 by Jim and Leila Frazier in honor of their friend.

Because of differing moisture conditions along the slope, the site supports a variety of woodland communities ranging from dry upland sandstone forest to small acidic seeps along the stream valley running through the site. There is also geological variation, with exposed sandstone, dolomite, and chert.

Typical canopy trees on the preserve include white oak, red oak, and shortleaf pine. Other notable plants include azalea, yellow ladies slipper, fire pink, fly poison, golden seal, purple twayblade, and marginal shield fern.

Of interest are several small seepage areas at the base of the slope; these acid seeps consist of small groundwater seep points emerging from sandstone bedding planes in the stream bed. Typical plants associated with these seeps include wild hydrangea, spice bush, Christmas fern, broad beech fern, water pimpernel, and golden ragwort as well as an Old World weed, watercress.

Nothing is known regarding the birds and other animals on the preserve. Any additional information compiled by preserve visitors would be helpful. If you visit during the spring be sure and stop at the nearby Alma Peterson Azalea Memorial (see page 97).

N. L. Williams Memorial Woods

N. L. WILLIAMS MEMORIAL WOODS

Douglas County 🌿 *40 Acres*

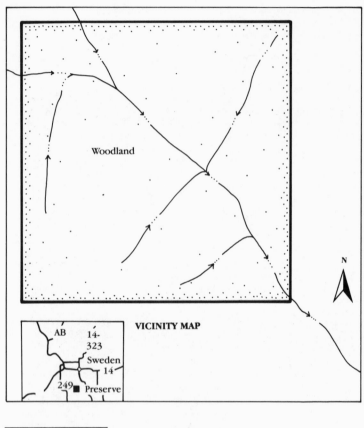

Woodland

VICINITY MAP

AB   14-
      323
      Sweden
        14
249 ■ Preserve

N

0   250'   500'

━━ Preserve Boundary   ⌇⌇ Drainage

LOCATION

Approximately one mile south of Sweden (Sec. 7, T25N, R14W, Douglas County).

DIRECTIONS

Williams Woods is located south of the small town of Sweden, southeast of Ava. The preserve is difficult to locate and requires crossing private property. Access is by permission only; please contact the Missouri Field Office at 2800 S. Brentwood, St. Louis, Missouri, 63144, (314) 968-1105.

USGS
TOPO MAP

Ava 15 minute quadrangle.

PROTECTED
NATURAL
FEATURES

Natural Communities: *Dry, dry-mesic, and mesic sandstone forest; acid seep.*
Species: *Fly poison, yellow lady's slipper, purple twayblade, azalea.*

BEST TIME
TO GO

Spring and fall, although summer visits will yield a surprising diversity of flowers.

HIKING
CONDITIONS

A map and compass are helpful to get in and out of the site.

Note that another preserve, Alma Peterson Azalea Memorial, is located approximately one mile from this site.

BENNETT SPRING SAVANNA

Missouri fishermen, campers, and canoers are familiar with Bennett Spring State Park, an upper Ozark paradise of scenic and recreational resources. Approximately six miles south of the park's border, on either side of Highway 00 in Laclede County, lie 160 acres of trees, wildflowers, grasses, and sedges that delight the senses and excite the imagination of visitors.

Look for an old dirt road on the east side of Highway 00, near a wooden sign announcing Bennett Spring Savanna, and park before the gate. The gate is set a few yards down the old road, so parking is limited to one or two vehicles. This tract was acquired by The Nature Conservancy in 1983, and is jointly managed with the Missouri Department of Natural Resources. It is the focus of intensive research into the workings of the savanna natural community.

The openness of the preserve, especially to the east of Highway 00, is striking. Here the scattered oaks and hickories raise full, gnarled canopies, while tall bottlebrush grass, Indian grass, and blazing stars wave beneath them. Few young trees and shrubs divert attention from the dramatic sight. They have been controlled through burning, as they were for thousands of years before European settlers tamed the Ozarks.

Along with veteran trees, fire-adapted grasses and forbs

characterize a savanna. These plants depend on strong sunlight, which they cannot receive under dense forest canopies. They thrive under the less-shaded conditions created when fires clear away the understory. This is illustrated by comparing the eastern fifty-five acres of Bennett Spring Savanna to its western 105 acres.

The western side didn't burn as often as the eastern side. In the interim, young trees and shrubs grew, creating a thick understory. Notice in summer that, without spring wildflowers, the ground layer is not as rich as on the eastern side.

The west-central section offers a varied terrain. The ravines and creek invite exploration. They might lead to shy turtles, delicate ferns, or elusive birds living above the thin cherty soil. When there is water in the creek, it cools tired feet on a hot summer day. Black hickories join with white, black, post, and blackjack oaks to provide shade. In autumn, the leaves present their color show, and in winter, visitors can pass among the trunks and marvel at the deceptive austerity that will soon be broken by birdsong and wildflowers. Deep in the ravines, it is easy to forget that the preserve is limited. Fences mark all four boundaries. One is never far from the highway, but a compass and topographic map will aid navigation in the more rugged sections of the preserve.

Several research projects are active on the site. Visitors might notice trees flagged to mark permanent plots used to monitor changes in woodland density and composition. Other trees are flagged and lines burned to indicate boundaries for prescribed fires. These controlled burns are designed to reveal how the restoration of an ancient force that shaped savannas will affect the current vegetation.

During each growing season, data about the vegetation in several areas of the preserve is gathered. This data provides an important avenue for understanding Ozark savannas. Land survey records, compiled in 1846, indicate that the Bennett Spring Savanna area supported widely spaced trees of the same species present today. Early explorers reported their awe of Ozark savannas when resplendent with flowers and grasses, and when ablaze. Through research and judicious management, Bennett Spring Savanna will retain the species and character valued by explorers then and now.

Bennett Spring Savanna

BENNETT SPRING SAVANNA

Laclede County 🌿 *160 Acres*

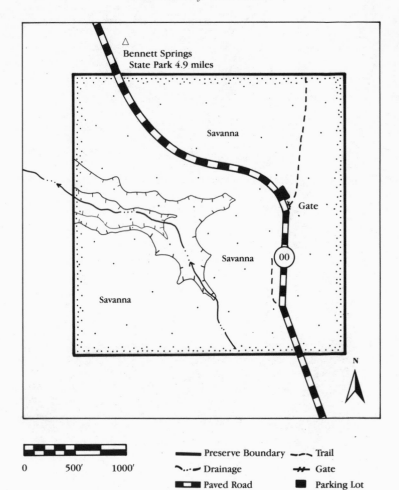

Bennett Springs
State Park 4.9 miles

Savanna

Gate

Savanna

00

Savanna

N

0   500'   1000'

—— Preserve Boundary ⌐⌐ Trail
⌐⌐ Drainage   ✠ Gate
▣ Paved Road   ■ Parking Lot

AT A GLANCE

LOCATION	*On either side of Highway 00, about six miles south of Bennett Spring State Park, north of Highway 32 (Sec. 18, T34N, R17W, Laclede County).*
DIRECTIONS	*From Lebanon in Laclede County, go west on Highway 64 toward Bennett Spring State Park. Travel west through the park on 64A; turn left onto Highway 00. Continue south on Highway 00 for six miles and look to the left (east) for the preserve sign. Park on the old dirt road that branches off of Highway 00 near the sign. A gate prevents further travel down the dirt road; the parking area can only accommodate one or two vehicles.*
USGS TOPO MAP	*Bennett Springs 7.5 minute quadrangle.*
PROTECTED NATURAL FEATURES	**Natural Community:** *Dry-mesic chert savanna.* **Species:** *Downy blue gentian, pink milkwort, royal catchfly, stiff aster, dogface and baltimore checkerspot butterflies, red milk snake.*
BEST TIME TO GO	*Late summer for grasses and flowers. Fall for colorful scenery. Winter for easy paths through the trees. Spring for wildflowers.*
HIKING CONDITIONS	*The terrain is steep near the ravines and the creek rises after rain.*

FIRE

Long viewed as a catastrophic, destructive force on the landscape, fire is increasingly being recognized as a natural process essential for the existence of many of Missouri's natural systems.

The role of fire in the pre-settlement landscape was ignored until very recently. Early settlers often actively suppressed fires in order to protect structures and improvements and foresters conducted public campaigns to reduce forest fires.

New research and a close examination of early explorers' and settlers' accounts in the state have revealed that Indian fires were a common, recurring, and widespread feature of the pre-settlement landscape. An 1859 account from the Ozark region is revealing:

"This stunted growth (the appearance of Ozark forests) is not, however, due to the poverty of the soil, but to fires which have annually overrun the country since the earliest dates of the Indian traditions."

Many changes that have taken place in our natural landscape since settlement can be attributed to the effects of fire suppression. To maintain Missouri's original biological diversity, it is necessary to maintain the spectrum of natural processes to which our rich

Points of Interest

natural heritage is adapted. The Conservancy is using fire as one natural management tool at several woodland, glade, and prairie sites throughout the state.

Controlled fire involves careful study and analysis to determine the pre-settlement character of an area, the management objectives, the current condition, and fuel load. This information is used to design a fire plan, which includes careful analysis of fire behaviors under various conditions, and results in a set of weather and fuel conditions which will produce the desired management objectives under safe and controllable conditions. Fire management on Conservancy preserves is conducted by specially trained and equipped burn crews working in conjunction with local fire control authorities.

On one of your visits to a Conservancy preserve, you may see the effects of a recent fire. Instead of viewing it as an undesirable destructive force, look closely and you will see it as a renewing natural process, making nutrients available, suppressing undesirable plant species, and promoting a more diverse assemblage of native plants and animals, including many of our rarest species. ❧

Fire

18

LICHEN GLADE

Lichen Glade consists of a large expanse of massive sandstone bluffs and bedrock along the east side of Salt Creek, in southwestern Missouri. The predominately west and south facing sandstone exposures, with large areas of bare rock and thin, sterile soils elsewhere, creates a harsh, sunbaked environment for plants and animals for much of the growing season.

Because of this, much of the preserve is a series of sandstone glades, with large patches of moss and lichen covered rocks. Islands of gnarled, stunted woody plants occur here and there throughout the glades, in areas of slightly deeper soils. Here increased moisture-holding capabilities allow trees and shrubs to gain a foothold. Trees growing on the glade are primarily small post oak, blackjack oak, and black hickory.

Sandstone glades have a characteristic and unique flora and fauna. The dominant grass through much of the glade is little bluestem, a species common in most prairies as well. Other characteristic plants include fame flower, widow's cross, false garlic, prickly pear cactus, and rattlebox. Extremely sterile, dry areas with almost nonexistent soil provide habitat for nits-and-lice, a plant with tiny orange flowers, hair sedge, rough buttonweed, and rushfoil.

The abundant areas of exposed rock are colonized by extensive colonies of lichens, especially the sea-green patches of *Xanthoparmelia*. Close inspection during the summer often reveals the presence of a well-camouflaged animal characteristic of sandstone glades—the lichen grasshopper. This insect is colored a mottled gray-green exactly resembling the lichens among which it lives. About the only way to locate lichen grasshoppers on Lichen Glade is to walk through suitable habitat, watching to see where the insects land when they have been flushed. Several types of lizards and snakes have been seen on the preserve, but very little is known regarding additional animal life.

Below the glade and bluff is a small floodplain forest along Salt Creek. Here, in a far moister and more nutrient-rich environment, a completely different natural community exists, characterized by trees such as river birch and elm. It is interesting to note the difference a few feet of vertical distance can have in determining the life forms inhabiting an area.

In recent years, Lichen Glade and other glades throughout Missouri have become overgrown with woody plants. If allowed to continue, this increase would result in the shading out and eventual elimination of much of the glade vegetation. Many local accounts correlate the increase in woody invasion with a cessation or reduction of fires in the area. Since it is known that Indians in Missouri regularly burned much of the landscape, portions of Lichen Glade are being managed with controlled fire to simulate this process and observe its effects both on woody encroachment and the glade life forms. The site is leased to the Missouri Department of Conservation and is a designated State Natural Area.

Lichen Glade

LICHEN GLADE

Saint Clair County 🙠 *29.6 Acres*

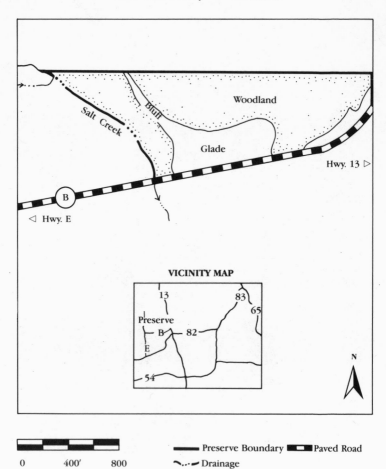

Woodland

Salt Creek

Bluff

Glade

Hwy. 13 ▷

B

◁ Hwy. E

VICINITY MAP

13

83

65

Preserve

B — 82

E

54

N

0   400′   800

——— Preserve Boundary ▪▫▪ Paved Road

⌁‥⌁ Drainage

° AT A GLANCE

LOCATION	*Approximately six miles west of Osceola (Sec. 16, T38N, R26W, Saint Clair County).*
DIRECTIONS	*From junction of Highways 13 and B (approximately twenty-two miles south of Clinton on Highway 13), proceed west on Highway B for approximately six miles. The preserve lies north of the road just before the Salt Creek crossing, and is marked with a sign.*
USGS TOPO MAP	*Monegaw Springs 7.5 minute quadrangle.*
PROTECTED NATURAL FEATURES	**Natural Communities:** *Sandstone glade, sandstone cliff.* **Species:** *Fame flower, prickly pear cactus, widow's cross, lichen grasshopper.*
BEST TIME TO GO	*Visitation at any time is rewarding. The highlights can be seen in less than an hour, but longer stays reveal interesting rock formations and new scenery.*
HIKING CONDITIONS	*Be cautious of uneven rock surfaces and loose fragments while hiking. The glade can be far warmer than the surrounding lands in mid-summer. Bring water and wear a wide-brimmed hat.*

19

NANCY B. ALTVATER CORRY FLATROCKS

Three hundred million years ago in southwestern Missouri, shallow, slow-flowing streams meandered over the flat landscape, carving multiple channels. In some areas, these braided freshwater channels deposited sands that eventually formed a unique type of sandstone. These rocks, called channel sandstones because of their origin in freshwater stream channels rather than oceans, are mineralogically and chemically unique.

Where these channel sandstone deposits outcrop on the Springfield Plateau, the specialized and harsh environment they create harbors a special natural community. Corry Flatrocks, west of Dadeville in Dade County, contains a large expanse of channel sandstone, giving rise to a channel sandstone glade. Within this glade is one of the largest known populations of *Geocarpon minimum*, a rare plant with no common name. Geocarpon occurs only in a few channel sandstone glades in southwestern Missouri, and at a very few sites in Arkansas.

Geocarpon is one of a number of plants specially adapted for life in the harsh glade environment. This tiny plant, often no more than an inch tall at maturity, appears in spring. The flowers are almost invisible, and colored like the rest of the plant. As the season progresses, the tiny, almost succulent-looking geocarpon plants turn a characteristic wine-red color, before producing seeds, dying, and withering. By late June, most plants have disappeared. The plant is an annual. Little is known about the life cycle of this cryptic wild-flower, although recent studies indicate that the seed transport, and perhaps even pollination, may be dependent upon water puddles on the impermeable sandstone bedrock of the glade. The plants usually occur in extremely thin soil pockets bordering open rock expanses, in areas with little other vegetation.

A visit to Corry Flatrocks immerses one into the special character of the channel sandstone glade. Besides several glades, portions of the preserve are former pasture and upland woods. Even here, however, the thin, excessively-drained sandy soils and abundance of plants adapted to sterile, acidic environments testify to the special conditions at the site. On the extensive bedrock expanses of the glade itself, large areas of bare rock are interspersed with zones of mosses and lichens, as well as patches of flowering plants. Mixed with these mosses are patches of spikemoss. Spikemoss is a tiny fern that is difficult to tell from moss at first glance. Slightly thicker soil pockets have a better developed vegetation, and scattered mounds and pockets support stunted woody plants, such as red cedar, black hickory, and winged elm.

Several unusual or restricted species of plants occur at the site, including violet collinsia, selenia, glade onion, large-flowered coreopsis, slender sandwort, hair sedge, rushfoil, quillwort, potato dandelion, Texas saxifrage, and widow's cross. Numerous insects, including lichen grasshoppers and a variety of butterflies, occur here, as well as several species of lizards.

Nancy B. Altvater Corry Flatrocks

NANCY B. ALTVATER CORRY FLATROCKS

Dade County 🦋 *40 Acres*

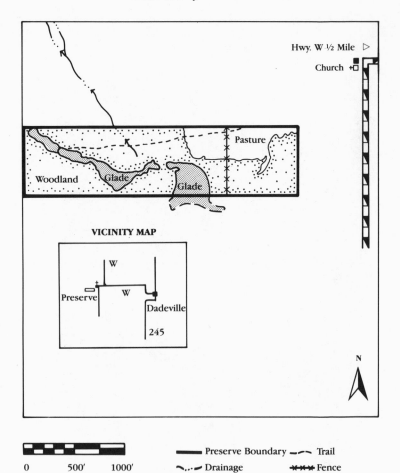

Hwy. W ½ Mile ▷

Church

Pasture

Woodland

Glade

Glade

VICINITY MAP

W

Preserve

W

Dadeville

245

N

──── Preserve Boundary	──⌐ Trail	
⌐··⌐ Drainage	✕✕✕ Fence	
⬛▱⬛ Gravel Road	⬛ Parking Lot	

0   500′   1000′

LOCATION
Approximately three miles west of Dadeville, west of Corry Church (Sec. 25, T32N, R26W, Dade County).

DIRECTIONS
Access to Corry Flatrocks is moderately difficult. The site is landlocked, and access requires a one-half mile hike over private land. For directions contact the Missouri Field Office at 2800 S. Brentwood, Saint Louis, Missouri, 63144, (314) 968-1105.

USGS
TOPO MAP
Dadeville 7.5 minute quadrangle.

PROTECTED
NATURAL
FEATURES
Natural Community: *Sandstone glade on Pennsylvanian channel sands deposits.*
Species: *Geocarpon, quillwort, violet collinsia, spikemoss, Texas saxifrage, lichen grasshopper.*

BEST TIME
TO GO
Early to mid May, when geocarpon is most visible in an average year. Late May to early June produces showy wildflower displays.

HIKING
CONDITIONS
Fairly rugged. Try to avoid stepping on the lichens that encrust the rocks in some areas; during hot, dry weather they become extremely fragile and are easily destroyed.

GEOCARPON

A *small plant in the carnation family* with no common name, *Geocarpon minimum*, grows only on a special type of sandstone in glades in southwestern Missouri, with a few outlying populations in Arkansas.

Since mature geocarpon plants are usually less than two inches tall, and the flowers are nearly invisible, they are easy to miss. They grow in very thin soil over sandstone bedrock, usually near the edge of open rock expanses where there is little competition from other plants. Geocarpon is restricted to glades on sandstones formed in the slow-flowing waters of ancient freshwater stream channels.

No mature plants exist on the glade in summer, only dormant seeds. By late fall, the seeds have

Points of Interest

germinated and produced minute rosettes, which overwinter, then rapidly grow to maturity the next spring. Geocarpon plants are tiny, branched, and have small fleshy leaves opposite each other on the stem. Erect flowers are produced at the tips of the branches, and are colored exactly like the rest of the plant. By late spring, the plants begin to assume a characteristic deep wine-red color. By early summer, they have produced seed, withered, and died.

Many questions remain unsolved about geocarpon, including how the plant is pollinated, how the seeds are dispersed, and how long the seeds can survive. It is thought that fall rainfall and water pooling on the impermeable sandstone surface may play a role in seed dispersal and breaking dormancy. Some researchers have also suggested that rainfall may play a role in pollination.

One of the best opportunities to view geocarpon is at the Conservancy's Corry Flatrocks preserve. Although the viewing season is rather short and very dependent on annual weather patterns, it is worth a trip to see this rare Missouri plant in flower. ❧

Geocarpon

20

GREENFIELD GLADE

At first glance, Greenfield Glade doesn't look like a typical nature preserve. Decades of human activity have erased many of the area's natural qualities. In fact, the presence of prickery brush, introduced weeds, and entangling vegetation can sometimes make this site seem downright unappealing.

In 1986, the owner of the land, Carthage Marble Company, donated forty-seven acres to the Conservancy. Seven acres were an outright gift. The remaining forty acres are managed as part of a long-term lease agreement with the company.

Yet, despite its lack of scenic beauty, Greenfield Glade Research Area does have something that makes it unique and worthy of preservation. It is home to a large population of one of the world's rarest plants: the Missouri bladderpod.

Usually less than eight inches tall, the delicate bladderpod plants are supremely adapted to the harsh environment of limestone glades like Greenfield Glade, one of fewer than fifty such sites on the planet. They are what scientists call classically rare, since they have both strict habitat requirements and a limited geographic range. In a good year, their tiny yellow flowers can be seen all over the glade from late April to mid May.

Greenfield Glade supports a mixture of open limestone glades interspersed between wooded areas consisting of young Osage orange, honey and black locust, and oak (post, black, red, and shingle) trees. The ground cover of the glade consists of both native warm-season grasses like bluestem and Indian grass and introduced weeds such as fescue and Kentucky bluegrass. Several showy flowering plants, including prickly pear cactus, beardtongue, and spiderwort, are also found here. A total of 277 native taxa and seventy exotic species are known from the site.

The Conservancy is working to restore the area to its presettlement condition by reducing the presence of woody vegetation and eliminating introduced weeds. Using prescribed fire may prove effective to open up the site and increase available bladderpod habitat. Several other research projects are being conducted at the site, including one to monitor the plant's population from year to year.

The gentle topography at Greenfield Glade allows easy access to the entire forty-seven acre preserve. Railroad tracks run through the southern half of the property; be prepared to cross two fences to reach the other side of the tracks. The preserve is bordered by fenced pasture on three sides, so there is little chance of wandering off Conservancy land.

Parking is available along the road at the north end of the property. A short trail heads south from the northeast corner to two old water-filled marble quarries. These quarries were active until the early 1900s and again briefly in the 1930s. When visiting the marble quarries, please use extreme caution. The area contains steep slopes, unstable rock piles, and deep, water-filled pits.

April is unquestionably the best time of year to visit the site. The bladderpod plants are nearly impossible to locate except when in bloom. Later in the growing season, plants like cat brier, nose-burn, and stickleaf lily, whose names almost inspire fear, dominate the area. Plan your trip for late April, but because of the sensitive nature of the protected plants and the ongoing research at this pre-serve, please contact the field office for permission first.

GREENFIELD GLADE

Dade County ❧ *47 Acres*

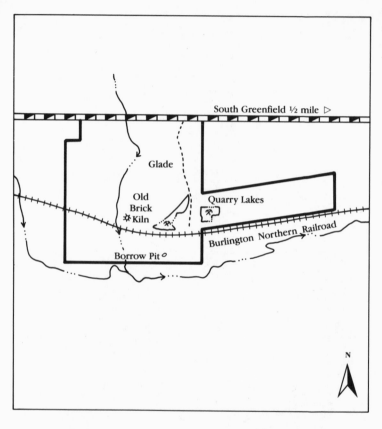

South Greenfield ½ mile ▷

Glade

Old
Brick
❋ Kiln

Quarry Lakes

Borrow Pit ○

Burlington Northern Railroad

N

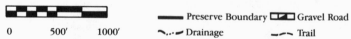

| 0 | 500' | 1000' |

——— Preserve Boundary   ☐☐ Gravel Road
～‥～ Drainage   ━～ Trail

AT A GLANCE

LOCATION   *Southwest of Greenfield, Missouri (Sec. 1, T30N, R27W, Dade County).*

DIRECTIONS   *Permission and directions can be obtained by contacting the Missouri Field Office at 2800 S. Brentwood, St. Louis, Missouri, 63144, (314) 968-1105.*

USGS   *South Greenfield 7.5 minute quadrangle.*
TOPO MAP

PROTECTED   **Natural Community:** *Limestone glade.*
NATURAL   **Species:** *Missouri bladderpod.*
FEATURES

BEST TIME   *Late April-mid May is the best time to view bladder-*
TO GO   *pod plants in bloom.*

HIKING   *Fairly easy, as the area is relatively flat. However,*
CONDITIONS   *brushy vegetation makes the area difficult to walk through during the growing season.*

MISSOURI BLADDERPOD

One of North America's rarest plants, Missouri bladderpod occurs only on limestone glades in a small region of southwestern Missouri, in the drainages and watersheds of six streams. These areas are subject to complete dryness in midsummer and saturated, frost-heaved conditions during the dormant season.

Missouri bladderpod is an annual plant, with individuals living only for a year, but it splits its existence over two calendar years. Seeds produced in early summer lie dormant on the glade until the wet, cool conditions of late fall, when they germinate. These seedlings form rosettes, or tiny clusters of leaves very close to the ground. The plants overwinter in this rosette form, remaining green all winter.

In early spring, the rosettes send up a flowering,

stem which is typically many-branched in healthy plants. By mid April these stems produce four-petaled yellow flowers at single points along the elongating flowering stalks. A robust plant may be six inches tall and produce hundreds of flowers. By late spring these flowers have been pollinated and produce the characteristic ball-shaped fruits, which give the plant its name. There are four seeds per fruit. As the dry hot summer weather envelopes the glade, the plants die, turn brown, and wither. The pods split in half and the two outer shells fall away with the seeds, leaving a white inner membrane on the plant. By midsummer, the plants are gone from the glade, and exist only as another crop of tiny seeds in the soil.

Surviving Missouri bladderpod populations experience large fluctuations in population size, with thousands of plants at a site in one year, and none the next. Little is known about the life cycle, germination history, ecological requirements, or insect pollinators of the plant. A crucial factor is how long seeds remain viable in the soil. Answers to these and other questions are vital to developing a successful management program for the bladderpod. ❧

Missouri Bladderpod

PRAIRIE

Prairies are open grasslands with little or no trees or shrubs. The word was apparently derived from the Latin "pratum" for meadow, and came into usage only in the seventeenth century as North American travelers attempted to describe the unique landscape they were encountering for the first time.

The roots of some prairie plants may penetrate the soil to a depth of fifteen feet or more. In such a manner, the plants are able to withstand the effects of frequent fires, which were a vital part of our pre-settlement prairies, or prolonged droughts.

Although more than 100 different species of grasses occur in Missouri prairie systems, relatively few species comprise the dominant aspect of the vegetation. Four grasses make up the bulk of the "grassiness" in all but the driest or wettest sites: big bluestem, little bluestem, Indian grass, and switch grass. Well-drained prairie sites on soils with a high calcium content are often characterized by side-oats grama, a distinctive grass with one-sided, pendant flowering spikes. Wet prairies are often dominated by a coarse growth of prairie cord grass, a tall grass sometimes reaching eight feet in height.

Points of Interest

Prairie

In addition to the grasses, more than 500 other species of flowering plants occur in Missouri prairies, including some of our most spectacular wildflowers. Some representative species characteristic of the prairie environment include rattlesnake master, lead plant, pale purple coneflower, white and purple prairie clovers, wild quinine, prairie blazing star, silky aster, showy goldenrod, and Indian paintbrush. In addition, several rare and endangered plants are restricted to prairies in Missouri, notably the prairie white-fringed orchid, a federally endangered species.

Birds, including rare species, are associated with Missouri prairies. Typical prairie birds include prairie chickens, upland sandpipers, short-eared owls, Henslow's sparrows, northern harriers, and scissor-tailed flycatchers. Numerous reptiles occur on prairies, such as the ornate box turtle, western slender glass lizard, and prairie kingsnake. Mammals include bison, badgers, coyotes, and plains pocket gopher.

Little is known about the largest and most diverse group of prairie animals—the insects, but there are a number of obligate prairie insects, including some of our showiest butterflies.

Prairies are adapted to regular fire. These fires burn off old vegetation, preventing a choking litter accumulation. They also serve to recycle nutrients and the blackened ground allows early soil warming in spring. In the absence of fire, prairies are invaded by weedy brush and tree species, with an eventual elimination of the prairie vegetation. Other factors influencing prairie vegetation include animal activity, particularly the actions of large grazers such as bison.

Modern prairie management is increasingly using frequent controlled burns to emulate the pervasive Indian induced fires that characterized Missouri's pre-settlement prairie systems. Other management techniques include cattle grazing to simulate the effect of native grazers, and haying.

Fourteen major types of prairie are recognized in Missouri, based on soil characters, topography, drainage, and moisture conditions. Within each of these types is a range of expressions that renders each prairie unique unto itself and truly irreplaceable as a component of Missouri's natural landscape. ❧

Prairie

21

ROCKHILL PRAIRIE

When the first land surveyor walked near what is now Rockhill Prairie in November 1837, he described the open ground as "rolling, stony, and fit for cultivation." He also noted and mapped the main wagon trail from Springfield to Kickapoo; this is now the small dirt road along the eastern boundary of the preserve. Concerned only with fulfilling the terms of his government contract, the surveyor had no sense that this treeless expanse of rolling land would one day be unique. Indeed, he had undoubtedly surveyed hundreds of acres like it in the past, for much of presettlement Missouri was open prairie.

Today Rockhill Prairie Preserve is nearly all that remains of Missouri's dry chert grasslands. It was discovered during a natural areas inventory in 1984 and was acquired by the Conservancy in 1988. The Missouri Chapter owns and manages sixty-eight acres at the site.

In addition to hosting 274 different plant species, Rockhill Prairie supports a population of the federally endangered Mead's milkweed. Notable plants include blue wild indigo, purple prairie clover, yellow coneflower, downy blue gentian, prairie parsley, New Jersey tea, and showy goldenrod. Two plants typically found only on glades have been sighted: Missouri evening primrose and prairie dock.

In mid July, a large population of blazing star explodes into a

Rockhill Prairie

139

purple carpet over the prairie. Upper slopes here are characterized by a combination of prairie and glade plants, while plants typical of wetter areas occur in draws and at the base of gentle slopes.

The preserve is located southeast of the intersection of Highways 65 and BB north of Warsaw. It is easily accessible and lends itself well to hiking and nature study. Parking is available along the shoulder of Highway 65 or at the pull-off on Route BB. Please be cautious when parking in these areas. Traffic can be heavy on Highway 65 and visibility is limited on BB.

Of the sixty-eight acres that comprise the preserve, currently only about one third is open prairie. Decades of human activity and fire suppression have allowed woody vegetation to take over much of the site. Hardwood trees began to colonize the area in the 1930s and 1940s. More recently, since the cessation of haying, cedar trees have established their foothold on the prairie. The Conservancy is striving to turn back the clock on woody encroachment by reapplying frequent fire to the site, simulating the Indian fires that maintained the area in presettlement times. Carefully controlled prescribed burns are being conducted in order to restore the site to an open, treeless prairie like the one the surveyor described in 1837.

Dry chert prairies like Rockhill are characterized by well-drained, shallow soils on hard, weather-resistant chert bedrock or residuum. They tend to occur on south- and west-facing slopes, which maximizes their exposure to the sun. The drought conditions on these sites result in the development of a unique vegetation type. Big bluestem, little bluestem, sideoats grama, porcupine grass, and broomsedge dominate the gentle slopes.

Early evidence from Rockhill Prairie suggests that the Mead's milkweed population may be in jeopardy. Recent searches for this rare perennial have revealed that most of the plants here are sterile and not producing flowers. Further studies are being initiated to monitor the plant's status.

Rockhill Prairie supports a showy collection of wildflowers from April to October. Early summer is an excellent time to visit the area, if you don't mind ticks and chiggers, but visits during other times of the year are bound to be rewarding. Because of its small size, this preserve can be explored in two to three hours.

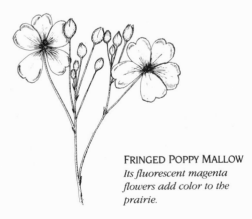

FRINGED POPPY MALLOW
*Its fluorescent magenta
flowers add color to the
prairie.*

ROCKHILL PRAIRIE

Benton County ✍ *68 Acres*

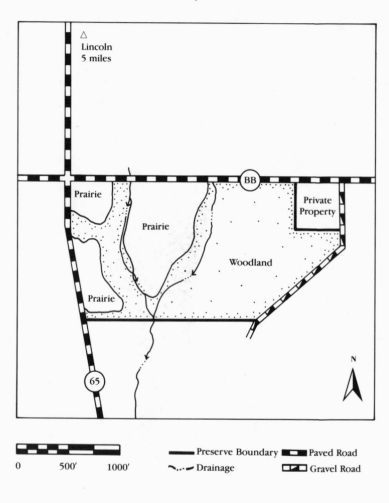

△
Lincoln
5 miles

BB

Prairie

Prairie

Prairie

Prairie

Woodland

Private
Property

65

N

0 500' 1000'	▬ Preserve Boundary ▭ Paved Road
	◥··◤ Drainage ▭▱ Gravel Road

LOCATION	*Approximately six miles north of Warsaw (Sec. 22, T41N, R22W, Benton County).*
DIRECTIONS	*Approximately six miles north of Warsaw, southeast of the intersection of Highways 65 and BB.*
USGS TOPO MAP	*Lincoln South East 7.5 minute quadrangle.*
PROTECTED NATURAL FEATURES	**Natural Community:** *Dry chert prairie.* **Species:** *Mead's milkweed, blue wild indigo, showy goldenrod, yellow coneflower, purple prairie clover, scurfy pea.*
BEST TIME TO GO	*Late spring for best vistas. In mid June, Mead's milkweed is most obvious. A variety of showy flowering plants are visible during most of the year.*
HIKING CONDITIONS	*Relatively flat and easy to explore.*

WAH'KON-TAH, MO-KO, AND
MONEGAW PRAIRIES

In southwestern Missouri, just east of the town of Eldorado Springs, are three of the Missouri Chapter's largest prairies. Here, large expanses of native prairie provide an unparalleled opportunity to experience the open, spectacular vistas that once characterized thousands of square miles in Missouri. All three sites are leased to the Missouri Department of Conservation.

Monegaw Prairie, the southernmost of the three tracts, consists of 180 acres just south of Highway 54. This rolling upland site with gentle, south-facing slopes, is officially classed as dry-mesic sandstone/shale prairie. A small draw runs north to south through the tract, and there are a small spring and artificial pond near the south end of the preserve.

Local areas of mesic to wet soils contribute to a high diversity of native plants here—over 220 species have been recorded at the site, including the federally-endangered Mead's milkweed. Animals of interest include upland sandpipers and scissor-tailed flycatchers, both of which breed here, as well as the rare prairie mole cricket.

Slightly north of Monegaw lies Mo-Ko prairie, a 416 acre preserve of predominately the same dry-mesic sandstone/shale prairie, but with a subtly different character and vegetation. The landscape here is more rolling, with low clusters of oaks and persimmons dotting the landscape. An extensive low rock exposure in the northeastern corner of the prairie produces glade-like conditions, and adds to the floristic diversity at the site. There is also an artificial pond near the south edge of the western half of the tract.

The prairie vegetation at Mo-Ko includes a wide variety of wildflowers, sedges, and grasses. Portions of the tract show the effects of past disturbance, and on a per area basis the vegetation is not as rich as Monegaw Prairie. Of interest is the presence of grass pink orchid. Animals at the site include scissor-tailed flycatchers, prairie chickens, and prairie mole crickets.

At 720 acres, Wah'Kon-Tah Prairie is the largest prairie preserve wholly owned by The Nature Conservancy in Missouri. Much of the area is dry-mesic prairie, with local zones of dry prairie. Cherty soils are prevalent over much of the site. Several endangered or otherwise noteworthy plants and animals occur here, including prairie chickens, Henslow's sparrows, upland sandpipers, prairie mole crickets, and Mead's milkweed.

Because of fire suppression and post-settlement disturbances, some regions of the prairie have degenerated to shrubby zones of low diversity. Future management efforts are designed to restore and rehabilitate the prairie community. Management at all three prairie preserves includes controlled burning, haying, and grazing.

The names of the preserves reflect and honor the cultural legacy of the Osage Indians, who formerly resided in the region. Monegaw was a latter day chief of the Osage who allegedly lived in the Monegaw Springs region. Wah'Kon-Tah means Great Spirit or Great Mystery, and Mo-Ko, medicine.

Wah'Kon-Tah, Mo-Ko, and Monegaw Prairies

WAH'KON-TAH PRAIRIE

Saint Clair County 🐾 *720 Acres*

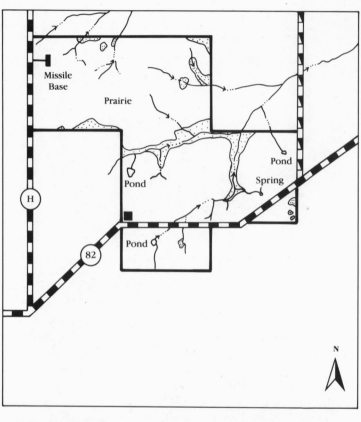

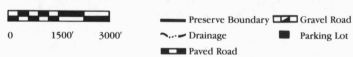

Preserve Boundary ⬛ Gravel Road

〜…〜 Drainage ⬛ Parking Lot

⬛ Paved Road

0   1500'   3000'

MO-KO PRAIRIE

Cedar County ❧ *416 Acres*

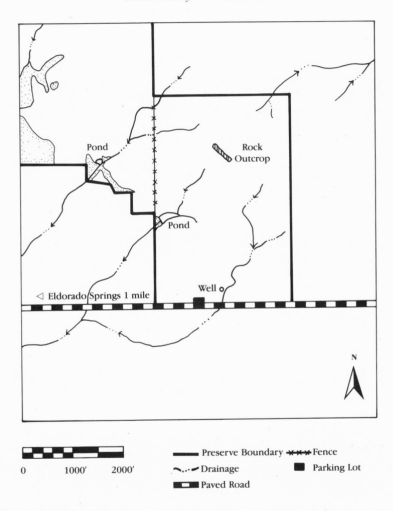

Pond

Rock
Outcrop

Pond

◁ Eldorado Springs 1 mile

Well ○

N

—— Preserve Boundary	✖-✖-✖ Fence
◟··◞ Drainage	▪ Parking Lot
▭ Paved Road	

0   1000'   2000'

MONEGAW PRAIRIE

Cedar County 🏵 *180 Acres*

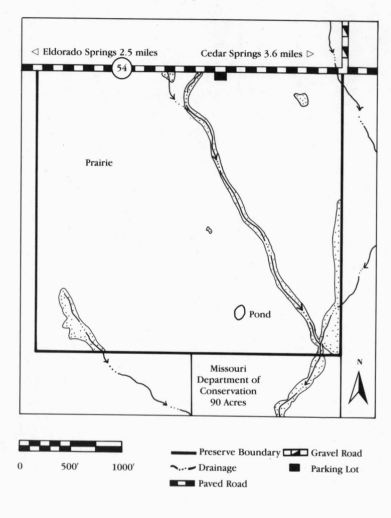

◁ Eldorado Springs 2.5 miles   Cedar Springs 3.6 miles ▷

54

Prairie

O Pond

Missouri
Department of
Conservation
90 Acres

N

Preserve Boundary ▭ Gravel Road

Drainage   ■ Parking Lot

Paved Road

0   500'   1000'

AT A GLANCE

LOCATION

North and east of Eldorado Springs (Monegaw: Sec. 25, T36N, R28W, Cedar County; Mo-Ko: Sec. 14, 15, and 23, T36N, R28W, Cedar County; Wah'Kon-Tah: Sec. 2, 3, 10, and 11, T36N, R28W, Saint Clair County).

DIRECTIONS

All three sites are located just east of the town of Eldorado Springs. Monegaw Prairie is south of Highway 54, approximately three miles east of the junction of Highways 54 and 82 in downtown Eldorado Springs. Mo-Ko Prairie is located approximately two miles northwest of Monegaw, and is best reached by proceeding two miles east of the junction of Highways 82 and H north of Eldorado Springs, then turning south (right) onto another gravel road for 1.5 miles, then turning west (right) onto a road for approximately 0.7 miles to the sign at the south end of the preserve. Wah'Kon-Tah Prairie is about 1.5 miles north of Eldorado Springs, north of Highway 82 about 0.8 miles east of the junction with Highway H.

USGS TOPO MAP

Monegaw is on the Filley 7.5 minute quadrangle; Mo-Ko and Wah'Kon-Tah are each on the Tiffin and Eldorado Springs North 7.5 minute quadrangles.

PROTECTED NATURAL FEATURES

Natural Communities: *Dry-mesic sandstone/shale prairie, dry-mesic chert prairie.*
Species: *Scissor-tailed flycatcher, upland sandpiper, prairie chicken, Henslow's sparrow, prairie mole cricket, Mead's milkweed, grass pink orchid.*

BEST TIME
TO GO

Early summer and late fall, although summer visits are often good for prairie wildlife. Some areas may be hayed by late summer.

HIKING
CONDITIONS

Hikers in the interiors of the prairies should have a compass; topographic maps are helpful to locate features of interest. Insects and sun exposure should be guarded against.

PRAIRIE MOLE CRICKET

While deer, buffalo, and jack rabbits graze on the tallgrass prairie from above, mole crickets graze from below on the roots of little bluestem. Prairie mole crickets are unusual insects, specially adapted to living in prairie sod. Their hind legs are not modified for jumping as in other grasshoppers and crickets. Instead, their forelegs have developed into strong claws, perfectly suited for tunneling in the soil.

Prairie mole crickets are large, up to two and a half inches long. They are a rich brown color, with short gold fuzz on the throat. The cylindrical body is streamlined, an important characteristic for an animal that moves about through narrow tunnels underground. They are strong insects, feeding on plant roots, spiders, earthworms, and other insects.

You probably won't see one when you visit a tallgrass prairie because they live underground most of their life. After two or three years of growth they molt into adults. This is the only time they come to the surface — for courtship and mating. As soon as the soil warms up in the spring, male mole crickets excavate a small tunnel system at the soil surface. The entrance is funnel, or trumpet-shaped, and it is attached to a small

Prairie Mole Cricket

oval chamber. Every evening at dusk, males back into this oval chamber and rub their forewings together. The chirping-grinding sound is trumpeted across the prairie. When a large aggregation of males are calling, the sound can be detected over long distances. Female mole crickets are attracted to the aggregation of males

and fly toward the sound. They fly over the calling males and choose the loudest male for a mate, drop out of the air and crawl into the tunnel.

With the loss and fragmentation of tallgrass prairies, this species has become stranded on prairie islands. Some populations, like the one at Niawathe Prairie, are represented by several hundred calling males. Smaller populations may not persist.

Points of Interest

Fortunately, for prairie mole cricket populations in Missouri, the prairie preservation efforts of the last twenty-five years have extended a great deal of security to this species. This is not true in the rest of its current range where few or no populations are protected and managed. In fact, many prairies continue to be lost. Because of habitat loss and the uncertain future of many populations, the prairie mole cricket is listed rare in Missouri. It has been proposed for listing as a federally-threatened species. ᴥ

Prairie Mole Cricket

25

NIAWATHE PRAIRIE

N iawathe Prairie, jointly owned by the Con-

servancy and the Missouri Department of Conservation, is a prime

example of a dry-mesic upland prairie system. The Conservation

Department owns the central 160 acre square, while the Conserv-

ancy owns eighty acre parcels at the south and north ends of the

site. The entire area is managed as a single system. All of the Conser-

vation Department land and the north eighty acres of the Conserv-

ancy land is a State Natural Area.

Soils are shallow to moderate depth over much of this rolling

prairie expanse, with slopes in valleys and draws ranging from gen-

tle to fairly steep. Sandstone bedrock exposures outcrop locally

through the prairie, adding to the diversity of conditions afforded

plant and animal life. A large, flat, east-west ridge runs through the

center of the preserve. Impressive vistas of the surrounding prairie

landscape can be seen from the summit of the rise.

Small drainage draws on the northern and southern slopes of

this central ridge create wetter conditions on lower slopes, with

small patches of mesic prairie vegetation. A small artificial pond

exists in the southeastern part of the preserve.

Of special interest at Niawathe Prairie are a series of small, ele-

vated mounds from two to three feet high and eight to fifteen feet in diameter. These odd elevated areas, called prairie pimples, or mima mounds, are of uncertain origin. They are a recurring feature on many Missouri prairies. Several theories have been advanced to account for the origin of these mounds, but none have been definitively proven as the actual cause of the mounds. Among the various actions suggested as the cause of the mounds are burrowing animals, wind erosion, Indian activities, and ancient geological processes.

Vegetation at this site is well-developed and varied, with several hundred native plants, including lady's tresses orchid, Mead's milkweed, royal catchfly, and blue wild indigo. Animals at the site include prairie chicken, Henslow's sparrow, northern harrier, short-eared owl, and prairie mole cricket.

The name for the Niawathe Prairie is derived from the Osage Indian term for "life-giver."

NIAWATHE PRAIRIE

Dade County 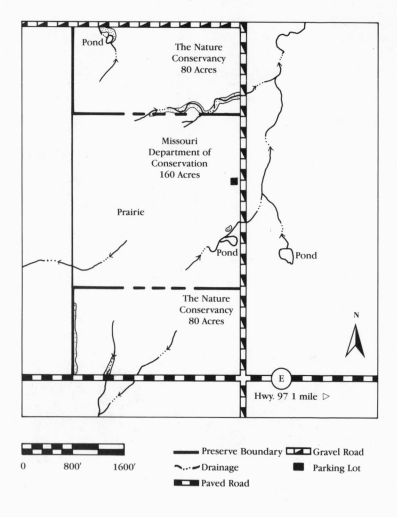 *160 Acres*

Pond

The Nature
Conservancy
80 Acres

Missouri
Department of
Conservation
160 Acres

Prairie

Pond

Pond

The Nature
Conservancy
80 Acres

N

E

Hwy. 97 1 mile ▷

0   800'   1600'

—— Preserve Boundary ▭ Gravel Road
∿··⌐ Drainage   ■ Parking Lot
▰▱ Paved Road

LOCATION — *Approximately nine miles north of Lockwood (Sec. 14, T32N, R28W, Dade County).*

DIRECTIONS — *From junction of Highways 97 and E (approximately eight miles northwest of Greenfield), go west on E for one mile, then turn north (right) onto gravel road, and go north for about 0.6 miles to sign and parking area on west (left) side of road. This parking area is on the Missouri Department of Conservation tract; Conservancy-owned portions of the prairie are at the north and south ends of tract. A gravel road runs along the north edge of the preserve.*

USGS TOPO MAP — *Cedarville 7.5 minute quadrangle.*

PROTECTED NATURAL FEATURES — **Natural Communities**: *Dry-mesic upland prairie, small areas of mesic prairie.* **Species**: *Prairie chicken, northern harrier, Henslow's sparrow, Prairie mole cricket, Mead's milkweed, royal catchfly.*

BEST TIME TO GO — *Early spring wildflowers such as Indian paintbrush are common here. Late spring to early summer visits are also good flora viewing times. Fall vistas are scenic. Parts of the prairie may be hayed some years.*

HIKING CONDITIONS — *Standard precautions should be taken to protect from biting pests and sun exposure.*

26

MOUNT VERNON PRAIRIE

For sheer size of a natural area, Mount Vernon Prairie has no claim to distinction. The forty acres protected here make this prairie small by most standards. But a visit to this site is likely to reinforce concerns about the loss of Missouri's native tall-grass prairie. Looking beyond the borders of this sanctuary to the farmland that surrounds it, it is difficult to envision the more than fifteen million acres of prairie landscape that once stretched across the state of Missouri.

Mount Vernon Prairie is located in the north central portion of Lawrence County about four miles northeast of the town of Mount Vernon. One of the Missouri Chapter's early acquisitions, it was purchased in 1974 with money from the group's very first fund-raising effort. The Missouri Department of Conservation currently manages Mount Vernon Prairie.

Despite its small size, Mount Vernon Prairie Natural Area exhibits a strong diversity of prairie forbs and grasses. The unusual-looking porcupine grass is common here, as are several other grasses including little bluestem, big bluestem and Indian grass.

Colorful species of flowering plants adorn the preserve in the spring, summer, and fall months. Blue wild indigo, downy blue gentian, leadplant, rattlesnake master, pale purple coneflower, fringed poppy mallow, and sky-blue aster are among the most notable.

In addition to protecting these characteristic prairie plants, Mount Vernon Prairie also serves as a refuge for animals such as the greater prairie chicken (now listed as endangered in Missouri) and the upland sandpiper. The ornate box turtle and leopard frog as well as numerous insects are found on this prairie. On one recent trip to the preserve, visitors observed three coyote pups peeking curiously out of their den.

Accessible and easy to explore in just a couple of hours, Mount Vernon Prairie is delightful to visit any time during the growing season. Parking is available in the lot at the southeast corner of the tract. There are no obstacles to getting around this site.

Mount Vernon Prairie

MOUNT VERNON PRAIRIE

Lawrence County 🪶 *40 Acres*

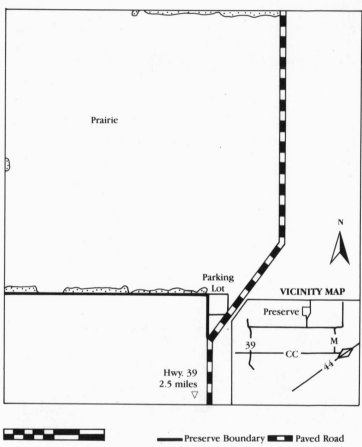

Prairie

Parking
Lot

VICINITY MAP

Preserve

N

39   CC   M

44

Hwy. 39
2.5 miles
▽

━━━ Preserve Boundary ▭▭▭ Paved Road

0   250'   500'

LOCATION   *Located four miles northeast of Mount Vernon
                    (Sec. 17, T28N, R26W, Lawrence County).*

DIRECTIONS   *From Mount Vernon, north on Highway 39 for
                    approximately one mile, east on Route CC for 1.2
                    miles and turn north. Proceed for one mile to the
                    first crossroads, turn east and follow the paved
                    road for about 0.9 mile. This road will turn sharply
                    to the north; follow it for about 0.3 mile to the park-
                    ing area on your left.*

USGS   *Miller 7.5 minute quadrangle.*
TOPO MAP

PROTECTED   **Natural Community**: *Dry prairie.*
NATURAL   **Species**: *Blue wild indigo, rattlesnake master,*
FEATURES   *sky-blue aster, greater prairie chicken, upland
                    sandpiper, leopard frog.*

BEST TIME   *Spring and early summer.*
TO GO

HIKING   *Accessible, flat, and easy to explore.*
CONDITIONS

27

WAH-SHA-SHE PRAIRIE

About one half mile from the Kansas state line in southwestern Missouri, Wah-Sha-She prairie is an example of one of Missouri's rarest prairie types. Termed hardpan prairie, this type of prairie is characterized by a unique vegetation and appearance.

Soils at the preserve are underlaid by a hardpan, or layer of clayey, impenetrable soils. Because this hardpan prevents subsurface drainage, hardpan prairies are saturated for much of the dormant season. As plant growth and warmer, drier weather develop in spring and summer, the prairie becomes a dry, sunbaked landscape. Plant root depths are limited by the hardpan, creating extremely droughty conditions for plant growth when the upper soil layer becomes dry. A short walk through the prairie reveals its differences from other, deeper soil prairie systems. Plant growth is locally sparse, and different in composition from other prairies.

This combination of excessively wet and excessively dry conditions results in an extremely harsh environment for plants growing in hardpan prairies. Little bluestem and switch grass dominate portions of the prairie, along with plants such as prairie blazing star, blue hearts, Indian paintbrush, large-flowered coreopsis, and chaffweed. Nearly 300 native plant species are known from the site. The endangered prairie mole cricket also occurs here.

An old artificial pond near the middle of the tract provides habitat for a variety of sedges and wetland plants, and may help buffer against lower summer water availability as a result of changes in adjacent land use. The name is derived from an Indian term for one of the subdivisions of the Hunkah meaning the Water People. Wah-Sha-She Prairie is leased to the Missouri Department of Conservation and is a State Natural Area.

WAH-SHA-SHE PRAIRIE

Jasper County ❧ *160 Acres*

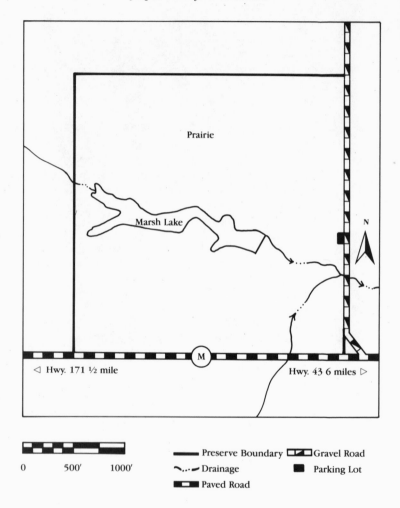

Prairie

Marsh Lake

N

M

◁ Hwy. 171 ½ mile

Hwy. 43 6 miles ▷

0   500'   1000'

—— Preserve Boundary   ▭▰▭ Gravel Road
◟⋯◜ Drainage   ▮ Parking Lot
▭▬▭ Paved Road

LOCATION
Approximately two miles north of the small town of Asbury, just east of the Kansas state line (Sec. 31, T30N, R33W, Jasper County).

DIRECTIONS
From junction of Highways M and 171 in extreme western Jasper County, go east on M for approximately 0.8 miles to first crossroad, then turn north (left) approximately 0.2 miles to parking lot and sign on west (left) side of road.

USGS
TOPO MAP
Asbury 7.5 minute quadrangle.

PROTECTED
NATURAL
FEATURES
Natural Community: *Hardpan prairie.*
Species: *Prairie mole cricket, various prairie wildflowers.*

BEST TIME
TO GO
Early to midsummer and fall are the best times to visit. Haying is used as a management tool on this prairie, so some areas may be mowed by mid summer in certain years.

HIKING
CONDITIONS
Standard precautions should be taken to protect from biting pests and sun exposure. Hikers during some seasons will get wet feet from the water retaining properties of the hardpan system.

HUNKAH AND TZI-SHO PRAIRIES

These two prairies, each a square 160 acre tract one-half mile on a side, are located within a half mile of each other. Adjacent to them are more than 3,000 additional acres of prairie within Prairie State Park. All of the tracts now making up the state park were originally acquired by the Conservancy and transferred to the Department of Natural Resources.

The names of the prairies are derived from Osage Indian terms for the grand divisions of their people; Hunkah refers to the Earth People and Tzi-Sho to the Sky People.

Hunkah Prairie is a very gently undulating, nearly level upland prairie on fine silty and sandy soils. Several low draws run through portions of the tract, with a small intermittent stream running through the northwest corner. Tzi-Sho Prairie, slightly east and north of Hunkah Prairie, is a rolling upland prairie with similar vegetation. Several small draws occur on the northern portions of Tzi-Sho, and pools of water remain here for all but the driest portions of the year.

Birds can be observed on the tracts, among them prairie chickens, upland sandpipers, Henslow's sparrows, northern harriers, and short-eared owls. Vegetation on both prairies is a diversity of upland prairie plants, with a blanket of typical prairie grasses.

These prairies are so close together, and adjacent to Prairie State Park, so that any visit should be planned to see the entire area and experience the Missouri prairie on the largest scale possible. Management of the prairies is by the Missouri Department of Conservation. Both preserves are State Natural Areas.

Hunkah and Tzi-Sho Prairies

HUNKAH AND TZI-SHO PRAIRIES

Barton County 🍂 *160 Acres Each*

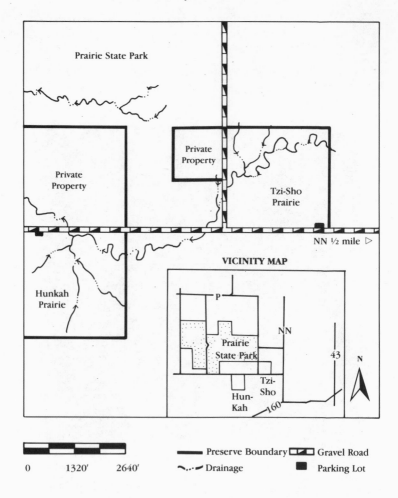

0   1320'   2640'

—— Preserve Boundary   ▭◢▭ Gravel Road
◝‥◞ Drainage   ■ Parking Lot

LOCATION

Approximately three miles southwest of Liberal and two miles northeast of Mindenmines (Hunkah: Sec. 27 and Tzi-Sho: Sec. 23, T32N, R33W, Barton County).

DIRECTIONS

From the junction of Highways 43 and 160, go west on Highway 160 for approximately two miles to Highway NN. Turn north (right) and travel one mile to the gravel road intersecting the Highway on the west (left). Turn west (left); the parking lot for Tzi-Sho will be on the north (right) in about 0.7 miles, and the parking lot for Hunkah will be on the south (left) about one mile beyond that. Both areas are marked with signs.

USGS
TOPO MAP

Liberal 7.5 minute quadrangle.

PROTECTED
NATURAL
FEATURES

Natural Communities: *Dry upland prairie, dry-mesic upland prairie.*
Species: *Upland sandpiper, prairie chicken, northern harrier, short-eared owl, Henslow's sparrow, numerous prairie wildflowers, prairie mole cricket.*

BEST TIME
TO GO

Late spring to early summer, and late fall. Haying occurs in late summer, therefore the prairies may be mowed.

HIKING
CONDITIONS

Be prepared for ticks, chiggers, and biting flies. Summer visits can be hot; bring water and avoid excess sun. Facilities are available in the Prairie State Park Nature Center.

UPLAND SANDPIPER

The *upland sandpiper, formerly called the upland plover,* is a bird of the upland prairies. In summer, it can be found in grasslands from Alaska south to Colorado, Oklahoma, and Virginia. The bird is uncommon in most parts of its breeding range, including Missouri, where it is listed as a Watch List species by the Missouri Department of Conservation.

Upland sandpipers are about a foot tall, with a wingspan of seventeen to twenty inches. Sexes are generally the same size, with brown, streaked plumage lacking conspicuous marks. Perhaps the most identifiable feature is the upland sandpiper's small, dove-like head above a long, thin neck.

Unlike most other sandpipers, the upland sandpiper is seldom seen near water. Instead, it prefers hayfields, meadows, rolling mixed-grass

Points of Interest

pastures, and prairies. Also unlike many of its relatives, it often perches on fence posts, telephone poles, and even in trees, where, after alighting, it holds its wings high above its back for a few seconds before folding them down.

Beginning about 1880, when the supply of passenger pigeons slaughtered by hunters for market began to decline, vast numbers of upland sandpipers were killed by market hunters. By the turn of the century in Missouri, hunting and conversion of grasslands to row crops had severely impacted the population. The upland sandpiper has never regained its former numbers, but can still be found throughout western and northern Missouri where suitable habitat is available.

Upland sandpipers show a preference for first-year burned areas (i.e., grasslands growing after a fall or winter fire has burned of the last season's dead grasses). Since the Conservancy burns portions of many of its prairies in early spring, these prairie preserves are ideal places to see this bird. Cook Meadow may be the best spot: on summer mornings the bird often sits on the preserve sign, easily seen from the road. ॐ

Upland Sandpiper

SHELTON L. COOK MEMORIAL MEADOW

Prior to settlement, at least a third of Missouri consisted of prairie. Although not common in much of the Ozarks and the bootheel, prairie was the dominant natural community in the northern and western portions of the state.

The west-central Missouri region, south of the Missouri River and west of the Ozarks, was Missouri's premium prairie region. Here, a greater percentage of land was in prairie than in any other part of the state. Often called the Osage prairie or Osage plains of Missouri, prairies extended over all the rolling uplands. Timber was restricted to the valleys, with narrow strips of open timber, called points, extending along drainageways into the upland prairies.

Of all the counties in Missouri, Barton County—located north of Joplin along the Kansas border—had the highest percentage of prairie, eighty-six percent or 511 square miles.

Very little undisturbed prairie remains in Barton County. In 1987, Monia Cook Morris willed a 280-acre Barton County prairie to the Conservancy in memory of her father, Shelton L. Cook. Shelton L. Cook Memorial Meadow, near Golden City, is an exceptionally high-quality example of this once widespread prairie. The gently rolling tract of dry-mesic prairie, interfingered with timber, is also habitat for two state-endangered plant species.

Cook Meadow Preserve has about 185 acres of prairie and ninety-five acres of woodland. The preserve exhibits an unusually high diversity of native plant species, with over 300 identified to date. An unusual feature of the preserve is a protected timber/prairie interface at the north end, along a line closely approximating that identified by the original land survey. This interface is one of the few in the state that still stands as it did prior to settlement.

Park along the county road on the western side of Cook Meadow Preserve, adjacent to the preserve sign. The sign is located near the top of a rolling hill, and the area yields an impressive view many miles to the south and west. Use the sign as the starting point for your explorations: it is visible from many parts of the preserve and so is a help in orientation.

The species of highest priority protected at Cook Meadow Preserve are Harvey's beak rush and fringed nutrush. Harvey's beak rush, a member of the sedge family, is found along the wet draws that flow south. The nutrush, a perennial grass, is more common on the higher ground of the prairie.

Cook Meadow is a good place to see the upland sandpiper, along with other typical birds of the region: scissor-tailed flycatchers, dickcissels, and Henslow's and vesper sparrows. Prairie chickens have not been sighted on the preserve, although they are known from Golden Prairie, two mlies to the southwest.

The woodland at the north end of the property is dense and overgrown and nearly impenetrable during the growing season. It has changed dramatically from presettlement descriptions, probably because of past disturbance and long periods of fire suppression. Although it will take many years, the Conservancy hopes to restore the woodland to its presettlement character: widely spaced trees with prairie grasses and forbs blanketing the ground beneath.

In 1987, the Conservancy initiated studies to determine the most appropriate way to manage the prairie system to protect the full diversity of species present. Cook Meadow has been hayed each summer for most of the last 100 years. Now, on a thirty-five acre section of prairie, annual prescribed burns are conducted to mimic the wildfires that once swept through the area. Each summer scientists compare samples of the vegetation of the burned area versus the hayed area. By 1993, they hope to understand the effects of various management treatments on site vegetation.

As you stand by the preserve sign looking to the south and west, remember that 200 years ago you might not have seen a single tree in those directions.

SHELTON L. COOK MEMORIAL MEADOW

Barton County 🐾 *280 Acres*

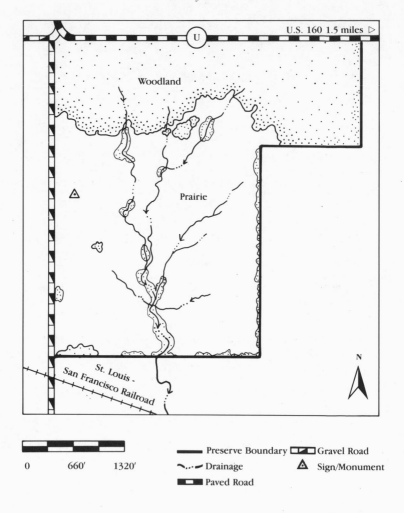

—— Preserve Boundary	▭◢▭ Gravel Road
～‥⌐ Drainage	▲ Sign/Monument
▭◨▬ Paved Road	

0   660′   1320′

AT A GLANCE

LOCATION

About 2.5 miles northwest of Golden City, Missouri, in southeastern Barton County (Sec. 21, T31N, R29W, Barton County).

DIRECTIONS

From Golden City in southeastern Barton County, go north on Highway 160 toward Lamar. After 1.75 miles, turn left onto County Highway U. Go two miles to the second gravel road; turn left here and go about 0.5 mile until you see the preserve sign in the prairie to your left. Park along the road adjacent to the sign, and step over the fence to enter the preserve.

USGS TOPO MAP

Kenoma and Golden City 7.5 minute quadrangles.

PROTECTED NATURAL FEATURES

Natural Community: *Dry-mesic prairie.*
Species: *Harvey's beak rush, fringed nutrush.*

BEST TIME TO GO

In spring and summer, flowers are in bloom and grasses are growing. Winter is the best season to walk around the woods.

HIKING CONDITIONS

Easy, over this gently rolling terrain, but clumps of prairie grass can turn an ankle. The prairie is generally dry, but water persists along the draws, and you may get your feet wet or muddy.

PAWHUSKA PRAIRIE

Within the seventy-seven acres of predomi-
nately dry-mesic upland prairie preserved at this site is a surprising
richness of natural features. Two small springs provide local wet
zones, increasing both plant and animal diversity. A small intermittent stream runs along the southwest corner of the tract. Two
former buffalo dusting sites occur on the tract, the last remnants of
the former presence of these powerful grazers.

A small sandstone ledge near one spring provides a shaded site
for ferns. In addition to the typical upland prairie flora, Pawhuska
Prairie has a population of Harvey's beak rush, a rare plant in the
sedge family. Coyotes, deer, and a variety of birds occur on the area.

The preserve name is derived from an Osage Indian term for
white-haired, a term used in reference to three Osage Chiefs. The
site is leased to the Missouri Department of Conservation.

PRAIRIE VIOLET
*A showy wildflower
restricted to high-quality
prairie sites.*

PAWHUSKA PRAIRIE

Barton County 🐾 *77 Acres*

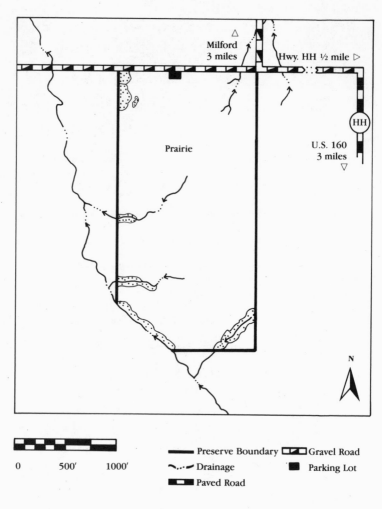

Milford
3 miles

Hwy. HH ½ mile ▷

Prairie

HH

U.S. 160
3 miles
▽

N

Preserve Boundary	**Gravel Road**
Drainage	**Parking Lot**
Paved Road	

0   500'   1000'

LOCATION   *Approximately nine miles east and slightly north of Lamar (Sec. 7, T32N, R29W, Barton County).*

DIRECTIONS   *From the junction of Highways 160 and HH (approximately eight miles east of Lamar), go three miles north to the end of HH, then turn west (left) on a gravel road. Go about 0.6 miles to the sign and parking area at the north end of the preserve.*

USGS
TOPO MAP   *Milford 7.5 minute quadrangle.*

PROTECTED
NATURAL
FEATURES   **Natural Community:** *Dry-mesic upland prairie.*
Species: *Harvey's beak rush.*

BEST TIME
TO GO   *Late spring and early summer provide good wildflower and bird viewing opportunities. Fall is also a scenic time to visit the preserve, although portions of the prairie may be hayed in some years.*

HIKING
CONDITIONS   *Standard precautions should be taken to protect from biting pests and sun exposure.*

32

LITTLE OSAGE PRAIRIE

This eighty-acre tract of dry-mesic prairie is located south of Nevada. Representative of the upland prairies that once covered the vast majority of this region of the state, Little Osage Prairie provides an opportunity to easily explore a prairie rich in plant species. Gently rolling slopes cover the entire site, providing ready access to the visitor. The site is leased to the Missouri Department of Conservation.

In addition to a rich assemblage of characteristic upland prairie plants, Mead's milkweed, a federally listed endangered species, occurs here. The rare prairie mole cricket is also known at the site.

INDIAN GRASS
A common grass of tall-grass prairies.

LITTLE OSAGE PRAIRIE

Vernon County ❧ *80 Acres*

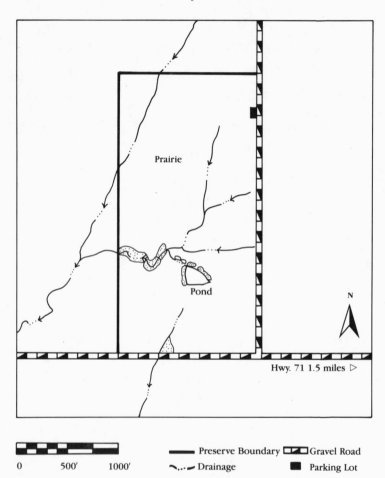

Prairie

Pond

N

Hwy. 71 1.5 miles ▷

0   500'   1000'

—— Preserve Boundary ▱▰▱ Gravel Road
◠...◡ Drainage   ▮ Parking Lot

LOCATION

Approximately four miles south of Nevada (Sec. 34, T35N, R31W, Vernon County).

DIRECTIONS

From junction of Highway 71 and BB in Nevada, go south on BB for approximately five miles, until BB makes a sharp turn to the west (right). At this point, continue straight south on a gravel road for another quarter mile, after which the road turns east (left). Go for about 1.5 miles, then turn north (left) onto another gravel road, and follow this for about 0.4 miles to the signed parking lot on the west (left).

USGS
TOPO MAP

Nevada 7.5 minute quadrangle.

PROTECTED
NATURAL
FEATURES

Natural Community: *Dry-mesic prairie.*
Species: *Mead's milkweed, prairie mole cricket.*

BEST TIME
TO GO

Late spring and early summer produce showy wildflower displays. Autumn produces an impressive sea of tall grass, in years when the preserve is not hayed.

HIKING
CONDITIONS

Hiking and access are very easy. Standard precautions should be taken against biting pests and sun exposure.

33

MARMATON RIVER BOTTOMS WET PRAIRIE

Wet prairie was once a common feature throughout most of Missouri except for the Ozark highlands. Because of the fertility of these areas, most were converted to agricultural use shortly after settlement of the state. Today, Marmaton River Bottoms Wet Prairie, near the town of Nevada in southwestern Missouri, is the largest known single expanse of unplowed wet prairie. At this 650-acre preserve, nearly 200 acres of intact wet prairie are interspersed with wet savanna and wet bottomland forest communities. A portion of the preserve was a gift from Mr. & Mrs. Joseph L. Rinehart of Nevada, Missouri.

Located along the west side of the Marmaton River, the preserve also contains two oxbow lakes, as well as several small sloughs. The 1844 land survey description for the site is revealing:

"Land level, bottom soil rich, but subject to inundations to the depth of five feet as appears by the drifted grass on the border of the upland timber, a thin growth of pin oak, hickory, pecan, undergrowth oak, hickory, plum, and other bushes common to the bottomland."

The description for the site is an apt one even today. The wet prairie areas are characterized by a dense growth of prairie cord grass, sometimes reaching six feet in height. Interspersed in this waving sea of grass are plants such as willow aster, smooth button-weed, Pitcher's leather flower, prairie milkweed, and numerous sedges and rushes. The deep, silty soils in the prairie remain saturated to wet for most of the year.

Surrounding the prairie areas is a woodland complex largely composed of former wet savanna communities, according to the original land survey. Today the best remnants are characterized by large groves of pecan, as well as kingnut hickory and bur oak. Ground cover plants here are diverse, such as swamp sedge, swamp dock, and violet cress. In areas close to the river where flooding and silting occur more frequently, woodlands are more closed, with silver maple, box elder, elm, pin oak, and hackberry.

Of special interest are the plants and animals associated with the sloughs and oxbow lakes. Both of Missouri's carnivorous aquatic plants, humped bladderwort and great bladderwort, grow here, as well as water purslane and great duckweed. Numerous water fowl and birds can be observed, including double-crested cormorants.

With the advent of settlement, agricultural activity along the upper portions of the Marmaton River has resulted in a severe impact on stream quality, and the river is now silt laden, erosive, and subject to increased flooding amplitudes. This has resulted in several impacts to the preserve, including an altered flood regime, increased silting, and downcutting of the stream channel. Two parts of the prairie are recovering from an abortive attempt to convert them to crop land in past years. Future plans for the site are aimed at correcting or reducing the impacts of these problems. Portions of the site are designated a State Natural Area.

MARMATON RIVER BOTTOMS WET PRAIRIE

Vernon County ❧ *568.2 Acres*

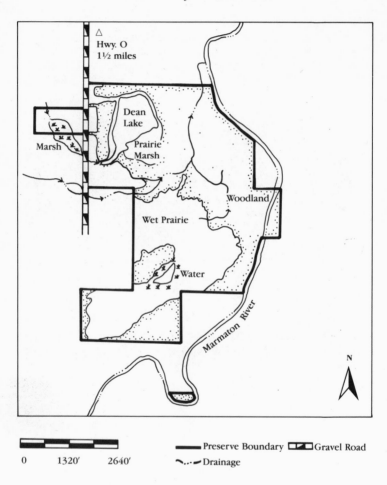

Hwy. O
1½ miles

Dean Lake

Marsh

Prairie Marsh

Woodland

Wet Prairie

Water

Marmaton River

N

0   1320'   2640'

Preserve Boundary ▭ Gravel Road

⌐⌐ Drainage

LOCATION

Approximately three miles northwest of downtown Nevada, along the west side of the Marmaton River (Sec. 18 & 19, T36N, R31W, and Sec. 13, T36N, R32W, Vernon County).

DIRECTIONS

From Nevada: from the intersection of Business Route 71 and State Highway W in downtown Nevada, proceed north on W (Ash Street) through town. About one-half mile after passing the state hospital on your left, W turns sharply west (left). Do not make this turn, but instead proceed straight on a small road continuing north. After one-mile, this road ends at a T junction—turn west (left). Follow this road through its twists and turns, over the Marmaton River Bridge, and continue west until the first road leading south (left)—proceed down this until you come to an abandoned white house on the west (right). You are at the north end of the preserve.

USGS
TOPO MAP

Metz 7.5 minute quadrangle.

PROTECTED
NATURAL
FEATURES

Natural Communities: *Wet prairie, wet savanna, wet bottomland forest.*
Species: *Small white aster, bur sedge, swamp sedge, Oklahoma sedge, turtlehead, violet cress, catchfly grass, swamp dock, double-crested cormorant.*

BEST TIME
TO GO

Early summer and mid fall. Prairie areas are managed by haying and may be mowed after midsummer.

AT A GLANCE

HIKING CONDITIONS
A compass is recommended due to dense vegetation, rugged terrain, and lack of trails. Be prepared for wet and muddy ground and mosquitos.

Note if there is standing flood water on any roads approaching the preserve, do not attempt to drive closer or walk to the site.

GREATER PRAIRIE-CHICKEN

*T*he Greater Prairie-chicken has not fared well
since the coming of European settlers to North
America, for the prairie it requires has largely been
taken over by agriculture. The eastern subspecies of
the bird, the heath hen, is extinct, and the Greater
Prairie-chicken, formerly a common resident of
midwestern tall-grass prairie, is now rare and
decreasing in Missouri.

Prairie-chickens grow up to a foot and a half long
and have a wingspread of twenty-eight inches. They
are generally brown, chicken-like birds, barred on
their upper parts with dark brown and buff, heavily
barred below. The short, rounded tail is black on the
male, barred on the female. Both sexes have blackish
feathers on each side of the throat; brownish heads
with a slight crest; fleshy, orange-colored eyebrows
(which are inconspicuous on females); and feathered
legs and feet with yellow toes. Males have bare
yellowish-orange "sacs" on the sides of the throat
called tympani, which are inflated in courtship.

Among the most colorful and spectacular
courtship displays of any in the animal kingdom are
those of the male prairie-chicken. In the spring, at

Greater Prairie-Chicken

early dawn, males gather in an area (called "leks" or dancing grounds) and strut or "dance" in courtship displays to attract females. These dances are filled with displays of plummage, the rapid stamping of feet, and the inflation of colorful throat sacs. The eerie sound made during the inflation of the air sacs is called "booming." The sound can be heard up to a mile away and resembles that made when one blows air across the top of an empty bottle.

The birds are year-round residents of the prairie, and originally occurred in much of the northern, west-central, and southwestern parts of Missouri. Local populations even occurred within the Ozark Plateau. Since the mid-1940s, prairie chickens have disappeared from much of northern Missouri, and some of the remainder of the previously occupied range as well. The decline in distribution and density has been caused by the destruction of permanent grassland habitat in these regions.

Large, permanent stands of grass are an essential requirement of prairie-chicken habitat. In prairies that are maintained by haying, trees tend to invade any unhayed area (such as along wet draws, or near

Points of Interest

sudden elevation changes). The trees provide a perch for raptors, which will quickly devour any nesting chickens within 150 yards of the perch.

Permanent prairie-chicken populations are known from Wah-Kon-Tah, Mo-Ko, Monegaw, Hunkah, Tzisho, Wah-Sha-She, and Niawathe prairies. 🌢

Greater Prairie-Chicken

34

GAMAGRASS MEADOWS

This eighty-acre prairie in southwestern Missouri is unusual in its deep, rich loamy soils. Soil depth in parts of the prairie exceed three feet. Most such prairies that exist in Missouri have been converted to agriculture.

Gamagrass Meadows is named for the abundance of eastern gamagrass on the site. This tall, stately grass, a distant relative of corn, is a characteristic feature of the prairie. The nearly level tract is dissected by three shallow draws. These draws are now densely overgrown with woody vegetation as a result of post-settlement impacts. At one time, regular fires swept through the area and prevented the growth of dense woody vegetation. With settlement, this prairie, like many others in southwestern Missouri, was used for generations as a hay source. The uplands were hayed, preventing the growth of trees and brush even in the absence of fire. Since the draws were no longer burned and were not hayed, they became overgrown.

In addition to gamagrass, other notable plants at Gamagrass Meadows include prairie larkspur, bunch flower, downy blue gentian, prairie parsley, and an unusual plant in the celery family with no common name, *Perideridia americana*. Dickcissels are common on the prairie in summer.

Gamagrass Meadows is a unique facet of Missouri's prairie heritage. A visit to the preserve quickly reveals the moist, lush aspect of this site, as a result of the deep, loamy soils. The area is leased to the Missouri Department of Conservation.

GAMAGRASS MEADOWS

Vernon County ❧ *80 Acres*

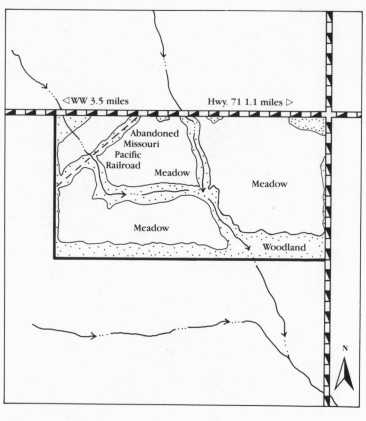

◁WW 3.5 miles

Hwy. 71 1.1 miles ▷

Abandoned
Missouri
Pacific
Railroad

Meadow

Meadow

Meadow

Woodland

N

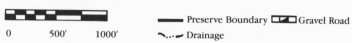

0   500′   1000′

—— Preserve Boundary   ▭ Gravel Road

⌐··⌐ Drainage

LOCATION
Approximately thirteen miles north of Nevada, one mile west of Highway 71 (Sec. 1, T37W, R32W, Vernon County).

DIRECTIONS
From Nevada, go north on Highway 71 approximately twelve miles to the small town of Arthur, then north approximately 0.9 miles to the next intersection. Turn west (left) and travel one mile to the next intersection. The prairie extends for one-half mile along the south side of the road running west, and for one quarter mile along the west side of the road running south. An abandoned railroad track bed crosses the northwest corner of the tract.

USGS
TOPO MAP
Sprague 7.5 minute quadrangle.

PROTECTED
NATURAL
FEATURES
Natural Communities: *Mesic sand/shale prairie, dry-mesic sand-shale prairie.*
Species: *Eastern gamagrass, bunch flower, prairie larkspur, Perideridia americana, dickcissel.*

BEST TIME
TO GO
Late spring and early summer are the best times to visit to see flowers and birds. Haying is used as a management tool on the site, so the prairie may be mowed in certain years.

HIKING
CONDITIONS
In some seasons, soil is soggy with temporary shallow puddles in low spots. Insect repellant is recommended.

The following alphabetical list includes all animal names mentioned in the text. For each name, the scientific name is provided.

———————⌒⌒————————

Badger, *Taxidea taxus,* 136

Bat, big brown, *Eptesicus fuscus,* 11

Bat, evening, *Nycticeius humeralis,* 11

Bat, gray, *Myotis grisescens,* 62

Bat, red, *Lasiurus borealis,* 11

Beaver, *Castor canadensis,* 58

Beetle (Tetraopes texanus), *Tetraopes texana,* 47

Bison, *Bison bison,* 136, 137

Bobcat, *Lynx rufus,* 83

Bunting, indigo, *Passerina cyanea,* 11

Bunting, painted, *Passerina ciris,* 32

Butterfly, Baltimore checkerspot, *Euphydryas phaeton ozarkae,* 109

Butterfly, dog face, *Zerene cesonia cesonia,* 109

Cormorant, double-crested, *Phalacrocorax auritus,* 190, 193

Cottontail, eastern, *Sylvilagus floridanus,* 52

Coyote, *Canis latrans,* 11, 136, 161, 181

Cricket, prairie mole, *Gryllotalpa major,* 145, 146, 151, 153, 157, 159, 164, 167, 171, 185, 187

Datana, great, *Datana major,* 53

Deer, *Odocoileus virginianus,* 11, 52, 181

Dickcissel, *Spiza americana,* 176, 198, 201

Flycatcher, great-crested, *Myiarchus crinitus,* 11

Flycatcher, scissor-tailed, *Tyrannus forficatus,* 136, 145, 146, 151, 176

Fox, red, *Vulpes fulva,* 11

Frog, green tree, *Hyla cinerea,* 70, 73

Frog, southern leopard, *Rana sphenocephala,* 161, 163

Frog, wood, *Rana sylvatica,* 58, 61

Gopher, plains pocket, *Geomys bursarius,* 136

Grasshopper, lichen, *Trimerotropis saxatilis,* 31, 114, 117, 121, 123

Grosbeak, rose-breasted, *Pheucticus ludovicianus,* 10

Harrier, northern, *Circus cyaneus,* 136, 157, 159, 168, 171

Kingsnake, prairie, *Lampropeltis calligaster,* 136

Lizard, collared, *Crotaphytus collaris,* 31

Lizard, fence, *Sceloporus undulatus hyacinthinus,* 52

Lizard, western slender glass, *Ophisaurus attenuatus,* 136

Mole, *Scalopus aquaticus,* 11

Mouse, plains pocket, *Perognathus flavescens,* 6, 9

Opossum, *Didelphis marsupialis,* 52

Owl, short-eared, *Asio flammeus,* 136, 157, 168, 171

Prairie chicken, *Tympanuchus cupido,* 136, 146, 151, 157, 159, 161, 163, 168, 171, 176, 195, 196

Raccoon, *Procyon lotor,* 11, 52
Roadrunner, *Geococcyx
californianus,* 31
Salamander, four-toed, *Hemi-
dactylium scutatum,* 58, 61
Sandpiper, upland, *Bartramia
longicauda,* 136, 145, 146,
151, 161, 163, 168, 171,
172, 176
Scorpion, *Centuroides
vittatus,* 31, 47, 49
Snake, red milk, *Lampropeltis
triangulum syspila,* 109
Sparrow, Bachman's,
Aimophila aestivalis, 32
Sparrow, Henslow's,
Ammodramus henslowii,
136, 146, 151, 157, 159,
168, 171, 176
Sparrow, vesper, *Pooecetes
gramineus,* 176
Spider, black widow,
Latrodectus mactans, 47, 49
Tanager, scarlet, *Piranga
olivacea,* 10
Tarantula, *Dugesiella hentzi,* 31
Turkey, wild, *Meleagris
gallopavo,* 92
Turtle, ornate box, *Terrapene
ornata,* 136, 161
Turtle, three-toed, *Terrapene
carolina triunguis,* 52
Vole, pine, *Pitymys
pinetorum,* 11
Warbler, bay-breasted,
Dendroica castanea, 11
Warbler, chestnut-sided,
Dendroica pensylvanica, 11
Warbler, golden-winged,
Vermivora chrysoptera, 11
Warbler, magnolia, *Dendroica
magnolia,* 11
Warbler, nashville, *Vermivora
ruficapilla,* 11

Warbler, palm, *Dendroica
palmarum,* 11
Warbler, yellow-rumped,
Dendroica coronata, 11
Woodpecker, pileated,
Dryocopus pileatus, 52

PRESERVE GUIDE PLANT LIST

The following alphabetical list includes all plant names mentioned in the text. For each name, the scientific name of the plant is provided, following the nomenclature in Julian Steyermark's *Flora of Missouri* (1963). The following abbreviations are used to indicate the status of various plants in the list:

SW: state watch list
SR: state rare list
SE: state endangered list
NEW: new discovery for the state, not yet listed
INT: introduced weeds, not native to Missouri
FT: Federally listed as a threatened species -
FE: Federally listed as an endangered species

———————————

Agrimony, swamp, *Agrimonia parviflora,* 58
Alder, *Alnus serrulata,* 57, 58
Aloe, American, *Agave virginica,* 46, 49
Arrowleaved tear-thumb, *Polygonum sagittatum,* 58
Arrow-wood, downy, *Viburnum rafinesquianum,* 21
Ash, pumpkin, *Fraxinus tomentosa,* 70
Ash, white, *Fraxinus americana,* 86
Aster, New England, *Aster novae-angliae,* 58
Aster, purple, *Aster paludosus,* 92
Aster, silky, *Aster sericeus,* 136
Aster, sky blue, *Aster azureus,* 161, 163
Aster, small white, *Aster vimineus,* 193
Aster, stiff, *Aster ptarmicoides,* 109

Aster, willow, *Aster prealtus,* 190
Azalea, *Rhododendron roseum,* 51, 55, 97, 99, 100, 103
Beakrush, Harvey's, SE, *Rhynchospora harveyi,* 176, 179, 181, 183
Beardtongue, *Penstemon tubaeflorus,* 128
Bedstraw, Arkansas, *Galium arkansanum,* 52, 55
Bellflower, marsh, SE, *Campanula aparinoides,* 58, 61
Bellwort, large-flowered, *Uvularia grandiflora,* 92
Berry, partridge, *Mitchella repens,* 70
Birch, river, *Betula nigra,* 86, 114
Black gum, *Nyssa sylvatica,* 70, 86, 97

Black-eyed Susan, Missouri, *Rudbeckia missouriensis,* 46, 49, 92, 95

Bladdernut, *Staphylea trifolia,* 26, 86

Bladderpod, Missouri, FE, SE, *Lesquerella filiformis,* 127, 131, 132

Bladderwort, great, *Utricularia vulgaris,* 190

Bladderwort, humped, *Utricularia gibba,* 190

Blazing star, *Liatris squarrosa,* 46, 49, 105

Blazing star, prairie, *Liatris pycnostachya,* 136, 139, 164

Blue hearts, *Buchnera americana,* 164

Blueberry, lowbush, *Vaccinium vacillans,* 52, 97

Bluegrass, Kentucky, INT, *Poa pratensis,* 128

Bluestem, big, *Andropogon gerardii,* 58, 134, 141, 160

Bluestem, little, *Andropogon scoparius,* 36, 113, 128, 134, 141, 153, 160, 164

Box elder, *Acer negundo,* 91, 190

Brier, cat, *Smilax tamnoides hispida,* 129

Brier, sensitive, *Schrankia uncinata,* 86

Brome, nottaway, NEW, *Bromus nottowayanus,* 22, 25

Broomsedge, *Andropogon virginicus,* 141

Buckbrush, *Symphoricarpos orbiculatus,* 86

Bulrush, leafy, SW, *Scirpus polyphyllus,* 58

Bush, strawberry, *Euonymus americanus,* 70

Buttonbush, *Cephalanthus occidentalis,* 65

Buttonweed, rough, *Diodia teres,* 113

Buttonweed, smooth, *Spermacoce glabra,* 190

Cactus, prickly pear, *Opuntia compressa,* 30, 36, 113, 117, 128

Carex abscondita, NEW, *Carex abscondita,* 70, 73

Catchfly, royal, SW, *Silene regia,* 109, 157, 159

Cedar, red, *Juniperus virginiana,* 120

Chaffweed, *Centunculus minimus,* 164

Clearweed, *Pilea pumila,* 91, 95

Cliff-Brake, purple, *Pellaea atropurpurea,* 86

Clover, purple prairie, *Petalostemum purpureum,* 136, 139

Clover, white prairie, *Petalostemum candidum,* 136

Clubmoss, shining, *Lycopodium lucidulum,* 36, 39

Coffee tree, Kentucky, *Gymnocladus dioica,* 10

Cohosh, black, *Cimicifuga racemosa,* 52, 55

Collinsia, violet, *Collinsia violacea,* 120, 123

Coneflower, pale purple, *Echinacea pallida,* 136, 143, 160

Coneflower, purple, *Echinacea purpurea,* 37

Coneflower, yellow, *Echinacea paradoxa,* 139, 143

Cordgrass, prairie, *Spartina pectinata,* 58, 134, 189

Coreopsis, large-flowered, *Coreopsis grandiflora,* 121, 164

Coreopsis, tickseed, *Coreopsis tripteris,* 16

Pecan, *Carya illinoensis,* 190
Perideridia americana,
   Perideridia americana, 198,
   201
Persimmon, *Diospyros*
   virginiana, 146
Pimpernel, water, *Samolus*
   parviflorus, 100
Pimpernel, yellow, *Taenidia*
   integerrima, 16
Pine, shortleaf, *Pinus echinata,*
   58, 97, 100
Pink, fire, *Silene virginica,* 100
Pipe-vine, *Aristolochia*
   tomentosa, 70
Plantain, heart-leaf, SW,
   Plantago cordata, 36, 39,
   40, 58, 61
Poison, fly, *Amianthium*
   muscaetoxicum, 100, 103
Pondberry, SE, FE, *Lindera*
   melissifolium, 70, 73
Pondweed, ribbon-leaved,
   Potamogeton epihydrus
   nuttallii, 65, 67
Purslane, water, *Peplis*
   diandra, 190
Quillwort, *Isoetes butleri,* 121,
   123
Quillwort, Engelmann's,
   Isoetes engelmannii, 65, 67
Quinine, wild, *Parthenium*
   integrifolium, 136
Ragwort, golden, *Senecio*
   aureus, 100
Rattlebox, *Crotalaria*
   sagittalis, 113
Rattlesnake master, *Eryngium*
   yuccifolium, 86, 136, 160, 163
Rock satin grass, *Muhlenbergia*
   sobolifera, 6, 9
Rose, swamp, *Rosa palustris,*
   65, 67
Rue, goat's, *Tephrosia*
   virginiana, 52, 86

Rush, scouring, *Equisetum*
   hyemale, 10
Rushfoil, *Crotonopsis elliptica,*
   36, 113, 121
Rye, Virginia wild, *Elymus*
   virginicus, 26, 29, 91, 95
Sandwort, slender, *Arenaria*
   patula, 121
Saxifrage, Texas, *Saxifraga*
   texana, 121, 123
Sedge, bur, *Carex grayii,* 193
Sedge, epiphytic, SW, *Carex*
   decomposita, 65, 67
Sedge, hair, *Bulbostylis*
   capillaris, 113, 121
Sedge, Oklahoma, SW, *Carex*
   oklahomensis, 193
Sedge, Pennsylania, *Carex*
   pensylvanica, 22
Sedge, savanna, SW, *Carex*
   swanii, 73
Sedge, swamp, *Carex*
   muskinghamensis, 190, 193
Sedge, tussock, SR, *Carex*
   stricta, 58, 61, 80
Selenia, *Selenia aurea,* 120
Serviceberry, *Amelanchier*
   arborea, 86, 92
Skeleton plant, SE, *Lygodesmia*
   juncea, 6, 9
Snakeroot, Virginia,
   Aristolochia serpentaria, 86
Snowbell, *Styrax americana,* 70
Spicebush, *Lindera benzoin,*
   70, 100
Spiderwort, *Tradescantia*
   ohiensis, 10, 128
Spiderwort, Tharp's,
   Tradescantia tharpii, 126
Spiderwort, Virginia,
   Tradescantia virginiana, 26
Spikemoss, *Selaginella*
   rupestris, 37, 39, 120, 123
Spleenwort, ebony, *Asplenium*
   platyneuron, 52, 86

FURTHER READING

Amphibians & Reptiles

The Amphibians and Reptiles of Missouri, by Tom R. Johnson. Missouri Dept. of Conservation, 1987.

Fish

The Fishes of Missouri, by William L. Pflieger. Missouri Department of Conservation, 1975.

Insects

Butterflies and Moths of Missouri, by J. Richard and Joan E. Heitzman. Missouri Department of Conservation, 1975.

Plants

Missouri Wildflowers, by Edgar Denison. Missouri Department of Conservation, 1978.

Flora of Missouri, by Julian A. Steyermark. Iowa State University Press, 1963.

Missouri Natural Communities

The Terrestrial Natural Communities of Missouri, by Paul W. Nelson. Missouri Natural Areas Committee, 1985.

CREDITS